To —————————————————

From —————————————————

My Favorite Recipe:

Signed —————————————————

Date —————————————————

About The Authors

JOYCE LaFRAY-YOUNG is the founder and publisher of Surfside Publishing, a young and dynamic company that focuses on leisure lifestyles, dining out and gourmet cooking. In addition to receiving her Bachelor of Science degree from the University of Dayton (Ohio) she also studied at the University of Loyola in Rome, Italy. While abroad, she travelled all over the Continent sampling favorite cuisines from many countries. She then taught Health and Physical Education for several years before working as an Account Executive for several major radio stations. Cooking and dining out have always been her favorite hobbies along with an avid love of tennis and outdoor sports. She holds many professional affiliations in the Tampa Bay area, is host of the weekly PM MAGAZINE food review segment "The Florida Gourmet" in Florida; consultant for the Burdine's Chefs' Tour for the past three years; member of the Florida Restaurant Association; and on the advisory committee for several local schools. She is married and has two children.

SUSAN SHEPARD arrived in Florida from Connecticut two years ago where she was actively involved with many different aspects of cuisine. She did publicity work for several cooking schools and caterers, wrote a restaurant review column for many years and was co-owner of "By Invitation Only," a party planning service. In addition, she's written many feature articles on foods for magazines. After marriage, Susan travelled extensively, her favorite pastime being to visit supermarkets and unusual restaurants. She resides in St. Petersburg with her husband and three children all of whom are interested in cooking, and eating — of course.

LAURA DeSALVO began her life-long interest in cooking at 17 when she was named Betty Crocker "Homemaker of Tomorrow." Since then she has travelled the globe, sampling foods from all over the world. While living for six years in Tokyo and Paris, she formally studied Japanese, Chinese and French cooking and attended the Académie du Vin in Paris. Married to an Italian-American and mother of two, she is currently perfecting her pesto and pasta. Laura and Susan work together in their firm, Editorial Associates.

The Underwater Gourmet™

THE GREAT SEAFOOD BOOK

Best
Seafood Recipes
from Florida's
Best Restaurants!

Cover Design By Tiffany Gullage

Winner Enterprises

International Standard Book No.: 0-932855-27-X
Library of Congress Card Catalog No.: 83-081849

FIRST PRINTING: September 1983
SECOND PRINTING: October 1983
THIRD PRINTING: November 1986
FOURTH PRINTING: August 1987
FIFTH PRINTING: July 1988
SIXTH PRINTING: April 1989
SEVENTH PRINTING: May 1990

PUBLISHER: Erwin Lampert
AUTHOR: Joyce LaFray-Young
With Laura DeSalvo & Susan Shepard
COVER DESIGN: Tiffany Gullage
ILLUSTRATIONS: Jack Emmert
TYPOGRAPHY: Hargett Graphics
DESIGN & LAYOUT: Michael Spurgeon

Many thanks to the restaurant owners, managers and chefs
who contributed their favorite recipes to this book.

Dear Seafood Enthusiast,

For as long as I can remember, I have always been a great lover of fish, shellfish and other "underwater" delights. While vacationing here, and after my migration from the North eight years ago to our fabulous Sunshine State, I became fascinated with the variety of seafood recipes from Florida's vast wealth of restaurants. My taste buds awakened an obsessive curiosity about how to select, prepare, cook and care for seafood.

I was determined to sample every type of seafood possible, especially those abundant in our Florida waters. The result of this lengthy search lies within the pages of **The Underwater Gourmet**™.

For each restaurant recipe selected, a dozen could have been, if time and space had been available. My choices were based on recommendations from many food editors and writers across the state, travelers, salespersons, media reps and many others. Criteria included great taste and ease of preparation. Together with editorial assistants Susan Shepard and Laura De Salvo, we researched, we wrote, we tested and tasted Florida's best cuisine.

I hope you enjoy **The Underwater Gourmet**™ with as much gusto and adventure as we have. I think you'll find it to be a most comprehensive collection of great seafood recipes.

So, get your face mask, snorkel and flippers unpacked. You're about to embark on your "underwater" tour of Florida!

Sincerely,

Joyce LaFray-Young

Notes From The Test Kitchen

In addition to the distinctive recipes included in this book we have provided some background and history on each of the various kinds of underwater creatures that populate the platter. So, when you sit down at the table, you will not only have delicious food to eat but food for conversation as well.

The recipes were carefully tested in our test kitchens. Some did not test easily and thus were not included in this book. We decided that if they didn't work for us, they wouldn't work for you.

Here are some suggestions for the cook:

- *Before marketing and planning your meal, read the recipe over CAREFULLY to eliminate surprises. One of our recipes has to marinate for 30 days!*
- *Some varieties of fish are hard to find fresh. Have an open mind and perhaps an alternate recipe when you shop. And, find yourself a good fish market where you can rely on their advice on what's best to buy when. They can be a tremendous help in fish cookery.*
- *Unless otherwise indicated, all the ingredients listed in these recipes should be the freshest you can find.*
- *Use lightly salted butter unless otherwise specified.*
- *Cooking and preparation times are approximate. Everyone works at a different speed, stoves (gas or electric) heat differently, and even the cooking utensils affect the timing.*
- *Ingredients are listed in the order that they will be used. We believe this is the easiest way to follow a recipe.*

Bon Appétit!

Susan Shepard
Laura DeSalvo
Joyce LaFray-Young

Dedication

This book is dedicated to my husband, Richard Young, and his family, whose confidence on this journey has helped to make The Underwater Gourmet a labor of love.

to all of Florida's restaurateurs who have made this book possible.

florida!

PENSACOLA
PANAMA CITY
TALLAHASSEE
GAINESVILLE
CEDAR KEY
OCALA
JACKSONVILLE
ORANGE PARK
ST. AUGUSTINE
DAYTONA BEACH
HOMOSASSA SPRINGS
TARPON SPRINGS
TAMPA
CLEARWATER
ST. PETERSBURG
PALMETTO
SARASOTA
ALTAMONTE SPRINGS
ORLANDO
AUBURNDALE
LAKE WALES
FORT PIERCE
CAPTIVA ISLAND
FORT MYERS
PALM BEACH
BOYNTON BEACH
DEERFIELD BEACH
FORT LAUDERDALE
NAPLES
MARCO ISLAND
MIAMI
KEY WEST
ISLAMORADA

"The pleasures of the table are for every man, of every land, and no matter of what place in history or society; they can be a part of all his other pleasures, and they last the longest, to console him when he has outlived the rest."

The Physiology of Taste
by
Jean Anthelme Brillat-Savarin

FROM THE PIER HOUSE MENU
KEY WEST, FLORIDA

Table Of Contents

T4-ABM-818

MULLET
MAMA

Salt Water Fin Fish

Fat and Lean Fish

Experienced fish cooks should be aware of the fat content of the myriad varieties of fish they prepare. The table at the end of this section categorizes many of the fish you may encounter.

Keep in mind the amount of the fat in the fish depends on the species, the season, and even the water depth where the fish are found.

In general:

Fat Fish

... have more oil in the flesh
... have darker flesh
... have a stronger flavor
... are well suited for broiling or baking
... need little extra fat or liquid to keep moist.

Lean Fish

... have oil concentrated in the liver
... have a more delicate flavor
... go well with sauces
... need basting when broiled or baked
... maintain quality during freezing up to six months.

How To Buy Fresh Fish

Here's what to look for when buying fresh fish:

Eyes	Bright, clear, and bulging
Gills	Bright red and free of slime
Flesh	Firm and elastic with exposed flesh appearing freshly cut with no traces of browning or drying out
Skin	Iridescent and unfaded, characteristic markings and colors clear
Odor	Fresh and mild with no disagreeable "fishy smell."

2

How To Buy Frozen Fish

Here's what to look for when buying frozen fish:

Flesh .... Solidly frozen, no discoloration, no freezer burn (white, dry appearance around edges)

Package ..... No ice crystals formed around inside of package or concentrated in one area. This could indicate moisture loss from fish flesh and could be the result of thawing and refreezing.

Wrappings ... Should be moisture and vapor-proof material with little or no airspace between fish and wrapping. Quality of fish is better if it is vacuum packed rather than overwrapped.

The following chart shows the edible percentage of fish in its various forms. Use this chart as a guide to determine which cut is more economical. For example, if the price per pound of fillets is no more than 55% higher than the price of whole fish, it is more economical to buy the fillets. Or if the fillets are no more than 50% higher than the price of the drawn fish, fillets are the better buy.

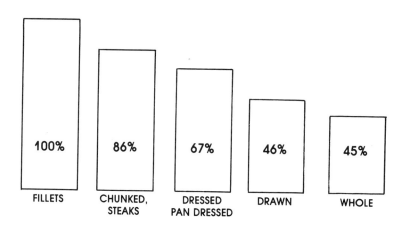

| 100% | 86% | 67% | 46% | 45% |
| FILLETS | CHUNKED, STEAKS | DRESSED PAN DRESSED | DRAWN | WHOLE |

To Serve Six People Buy:

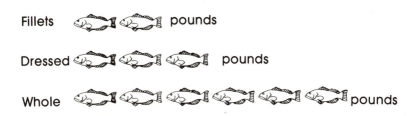

Fillets ⟨🐟⟩⟨🐟⟩ pounds

Dressed ⟨🐟⟩⟨🐟⟩⟨🐟⟩ pounds

Whole ⟨🐟⟩⟨🐟⟩⟨🐟⟩⟨🐟⟩⟨🐟⟩⟨🐟⟩ pounds

Notes On Cooking Fin Fish

Keep in mind that all fish are tender before they are cooked. The cooking process for fish is a flavor developer and a coagulant, not a tenderizing process as it is for other foods. The moment the flesh turns opaque and the fish flakes easily (separates or falls easily into its natural divisions) it is done.

Cooking time varies with the thickness and the size of the fish. To prevent overcooking, you should test the fish about halfway through the cooking time and frequently thereafter. Always test the thickest parts.

Before cooking, wash the fish thoroughly, dunk it well in salted water, and quickly dry inside and out. Lay fillets on paper towels and turn once or twice to dry.

Remember:

Pan frying
Best for fillets, fish sticks or small fish

Sautéing
Best for fillets, steaks, larger fish cut into cubes

Baking
Fine for all types of fish

Broiling
Fine for almost all types of fish except smaller ones

Steaming
Fine for almost all types of fish

Poaching
Fine for almost all types of fish

Planking
Best for whole dressed fish or fish steaks

4

Freezing

When freezing whole fish, make certain that the excess slime and internal blood is washed out of the body cavity. Freeze quickly at 0°F. or below in small, airtight packages. To help prevent rancidity and freezer burn, freeze fish in water in waxed cartons, ziplock bags or other containers. Another procedure is glazing. Package and freeze the fish until solid. Remove from freezer, unpack and dip the fish in ice cold water. Repack and return to the freezer. The contents will be covered with a glaze of ice which will further protect the flavor.

Thawing

Thaw in the refrigerator from 18 to 24 hours or place fish under cold running water. *Never* thaw at room temperature and *never* refreeze.

Sample Listing of Salt Water Fin Fishes and Their Fat Content

FAT
6 to 20% or more

Albacore
Bonito
Dogfish
Halibut (Greenland)
Herring
Mackerel (Atlantic)
Mackerel (Spanish)
Mullet, Striped
Pompano
Sablefish

Salmon (Pacific, Atlantic, Chinook, Coho, Red)
Sardines (Atlantic, Pacific)
Shad
Smelt
Spot
Trout, Rainbow (Steelhead)
Whitefish

INTERMEDIATE
2 to 6%

Alewife
Bass, Striped
Bluefish (Skipjack, Snapping Mackerel)
Butterfish (Gulf)
Croaker (Atlantic)
Herring (Pacific)
Jack Mackerel
Kingfish (Whiting)
Porgy
Sheepshead

Smelt
Swordfish
Trout, Brook (Atlantic)
Tuna, Bluefin (Horse Mackerel, Horse Tuna, Thon, Albacore)
Tuna, Yellowfin (Yellowtail, Tunny)
Weakfish (Shad, Trout, Sea Trout)
Whiting (Kingfish)
Weakfish
Yellowtail

LEAN
Less than 2%

Bass, Sea
Cod
Croaker, White, Yellowfin
 (Pacific)
Cusk
Drum (Atlantic)
Finnan Haddie
 (Smoked Haddock)
Flatfish (Winter Flounder, Fluke, Sole)
Grouper
Hake (Whiting)
Haddock
Halibut
Lingcod (Pacific)

Ocean Perch
Pike, Walleye
Pollack
Rockfish
Sea Trout
Snapper
Sturgeon
Sucker, White
Tautog (Blackfish, Chub,
 Oysterfish, Black Porgy,
 Moll)
Tilefish
Tomcod

GROUPER
SAUCE VIERGE

4	6 to 8 oz. grouper fillets
½	red onion, chopped
6	oz. white wine
½	carrot, sliced
	bay leaves
4	sprigs fresh parsley

—GROUPER—

1. Add all the ingredients, *except the grouper,* to a large pot. Add enough water so that the grouper will be covered and simmer for 5 minutes.
2. Add grouper and poach for 8 to 10 minutes or until the grouper is done.
3. Remove the grouper and serve with the Sauce Vierge.

—SAUCE VIERGE—

Combine all of the ingredients and marinate in the refrigerator for 1 to 2 days:

5-6	tomatoes, peeled, seeded, and chopped
⅕	bunch parsley, chopped
2	lemons, halved and thinly sliced
3	black peppercorns
3	tablespoons olive oil
⅓	clove garlic, skin intact and smashed
	salt and pepper
2-3	fresh basil leaves (or 1 teaspoon dried)

Serves: 4
Preparation: 30 minutes (plus 1 to 2 days for marinating)
Cooking: 10 minutes

"It is not vital for the sauce ingredients to marinate for 2 days, but the long marination does intensify the flavors. Top the fish with chopped parsley, and serve lemon wedges on the side."

GROUPER NIÇOISE

2	lbs. grouper fillets
	salt and white pepper
	Worcestershire sauce
	lemon juice
	anchovy oil (or paste)
6	tablespoons olive oil
4	cloves of garlic, chopped
6	ripe olives, sliced
8	green olives, sliced
4	large tomatoes, peeled, seeded, chopped
3	anchovy fillets
½	cup fish stock*
½	cup dry white wine
	chopped parsley

1. Preheat oven to 350°F.
2. Rinse grouper and pat dry.
3. Season with salt, white pepper, Worcestershire sauce, lemon juice, and anchovy oil.
4. In a medium-hot, oven-proof sauté pan, sauté the grouper in olive oil.
5. Turn over and place in oven until almost done (keep juicy and do not overcook).
6. Remove fish from pan and drain off oil.
7. To the same pan, add garlic and olives. Deglaze* with white wine and fish stock.
8. Add chopped fresh tomatoes and chopped anchovy fillets.
9. Put fish on top of mixture and let simmer for 2 minutes or until the fish is cooked.
10. Place fish on plate, cover with the Niçose garnish and sprinkle with chopped parsley.

Serve with boiled red potatoes. Add more anchovies and green olives.

*See glossary

Serves: 4 to 6
Preparation: 35 minutes
Cooking: 20 minutes

"Enjoy this at home or at the intimate Le Petite Fleur."

BAKED GROUPER PIQUANTE

1   lb. grouper fillets
     lemon juice
     olive oil
1   tablespoon Dijon mustard
     coarse dry bread crumbs
     melted butter
     water

1. Preheat the oven to 400°F.
2. Place the fillets, skin side down, in a flat buttered baking dish.
3. Sprinkle the fillets with lemon juice. Rub on a bit of olive oil; then spread the mustard evenly over the fish.
4. Sprinkle the bread crumbs over the fish; then drizzle with the melted butter. Do not moisten heavily.
5. Add a little water to the pan.
6. Bake for 12 to 18 minutes. Cooking time will depend on the thickness of the fish and the number of portions.

Serves: 2 to 4
Preparation: 10 minutes
Cooking: 12 to 18 minutes

"In place of the grouper, you can use snapper, sole or haddock with equally tasty results."

THE LOBSTER POT—REDINGTON SHORES

STUFFED BLACK GROUPER BOUQUETIERRE

1	black grouper (⅔ lb.)
	juice of ½ lemon
1	teaspoon Worcestershire sauce
3	cups plain bread croutons (crisp)
¼	cup finely diced celery
1	tablespoon finely diced scallions
½	cup hot milk
6	tablespoons butter, melted
	dash of nutmeg
	salt and fresh ground pepper to taste
	paprika
½	teaspoon thyme
2	cups chablis

—BOUQUETIERRE—

2	celery stalks cut in 3" pieces
2	carrots, in julienne*
1	small green pepper
1	tomato, peeled and quartered
	several flowerettes of broccoli

1. Preheat oven to 400°F.
2. Have fish filleted, leaving head and tail intact.
3. Marinate in lemon juice, Worcestershire sauce and salt.
4. To make stuffing, mix croutons, celery, onions, hot milk, 2 tablespoons melted butter, salt, pepper and nutmeg. Let stand for a few minutes but do not make a paste.
5. Put stuffing between fillets. Sprinkle generously with paprika.
6. Place in baking pan. Pour remaining butter over fish. Sprinkle with thyme, salt and pepper.
7. Arrange vegetables around stuffed fish. Add chablis and cover tightly with foil.
8. Bake for 35 minutes or until fish flakes.

*See glossary

Serves: 2
Preparation: 15 minutes (plus time for stuffing to stand)
Cooking: 35 minutes

"This is an impressive and delicious presentation."

11

GROUPER FLORENTINE

1½   lbs. frozen spinach, defrosted and well drained
1   medium onion, chopped
  salt and pepper
1   cup sherry
2   lbs. grouper fillets
3   cloves garlic, chopped
1   stick butter
4   oz. grated Cheddar cheese

1. Preheat oven to 350°F.
2. Combine spinach, onion, salt and pepper, and sherry. Place in the bottom of a large baking dish.
3. Place grouper on top of spinach.
4. Season with salt, pepper, garlic, and dot with butter.
5. Put in oven until 90% cooked.
6. Remove from oven and top with cheddar cheese sauce and grated cheese.
7. Put back into the oven until the cheese is melted.

—CHEESE SAUCE—

½   lb. margarine (or butter)
1   cup flour
4   cups milk
½   teaspoon salt
1   teaspoon white pepper
2   cups grated cheddar cheese
4   oz. sherry

1. Melt margarine.
2. Slowly add flour and stir constantly to make a roux.
3. Slowly add milk and whisk until smooth.
4. Add cheese and spices. Stir until cheese is melted.
5. Cook over low heat for about 10 minutes or until sauce is thick.
6. Stir in sherry.

Serves: 6
Preparation: 20 minutes
Cooking: 30 minutes

"Very, very rich and delicious. Not for those who are watching their cholesterol."

GROUPER ROCKEFELLER

1	lb. fresh spinach, thoroughly washed and stemmed
1½	cups clarified butter
¼	cup finely chopped onions
	salt, pepper and nutmeg to taste
½	cup heavy cream
3	lbs. fresh grouper fillets
	juice of 2 lemons
	flour for dusting fillets
2	oz. Pernod
1	cup hollandaise sauce*
	parsley and paprika for garnish

1. Preheat-oven to 350°F.
2. Blanch spinach in boiling water for 30 seconds. Drain well and chop finely.
3. In a skillet, cook onions in ½ cup clarified butter until onions are soft. Add spinach, salt, pepper, and nutmeg. Mix well and stir in cream.
4. Cook until sauce starts to thicken. Set aside and keep warm.
5. Make hollandaise sauce.
6. Season grouper with lemon juice, salt and pepper. Dust with flour.
7. Heat some of the butter in a hot sauté pan. Add grouper and cook until golden brown on one side. Turn and finish in oven until just done.
8. To serve, place 1/6 spinach mixture on each plate. Top with a fillet of grouper. Splash with Pernod and nap with hollandaise sauce. Garnish with parsley and a dash of paprika.

*See glossary

Serves: 6
Preparation: 20 minutes
Cooking: 30 minutes

"The Pernod is a special touch that makes this grouper quite special."

GROUPER PARMESAN

4	lbs. grouper, cut into 6 pieces
¼	cup lemon juice
2	pints sour cream (or imitation sour cream such as King Sour)
1	cup chopped red onions
¼	cup Worcestershire sauce
¼	cup cooking sherry
⅛	cup Parmesan cheese
⅛	cup chopped parsley

1. Bake fish at 350°F. in a lightly greased baking pan. This will take about 15 minutes.
2. While fish is cooking, mix the remaining ingredients together for the sauce.
3. In an oven-proof dish or baking pan, spread a thin coat of the sauce on the bottom.
4. Place the fish over the sauce, and pour the rest of the sauce over the fish.
5. Return to the oven just until sauce is heated through.

Serves: 6
Preparation: 10 minutes
Cooking: approximately 20 minutes

"Here's another innovative dish for our native grouper. Unless you are a true purist, use the imitation sour cream. The chef says it is easier to blend into the other ingredients."

14

FRIED GROUPER

4 grouper fillets
1 cup flour
1 cup milk
1 cup cracker meal
oil for deep fat frying

1. Cut grouper into strips about 1 inch wide. Dip in flour, then milk, then cracker meal.
2. Heat oil to 340°F. Fry until golden brown. Blot on paper towels and serve piping hot.

Serves: 4
Preparation: 5 minutes
Cooking: 5 to 10 minutes

"Moist and delicious."

GROUPER ROYAL

1	lb. sweet butter at room temperature.
½	cup light brown sugar
½	cup finely ground pecans
3	lbs. fresh grouper fillets (or enough for 6 persons) juice from 2 lemons salt and white pepper to taste
½	cup flour for dusting
1½	cups clarified butter* parsley for garnish

1. Combine butter, brown sugar and pecans. Mix until well blended. Set aside.
2. Season grouper with lemon juice, salt and pepper. Dust lightly with flour.
3. Put clarified butter and grouper in a hot sauté pan. Cook until fish is golden brown on one side. Turn the fillets. Cover and finish cooking on low heat.
4. Remove fish to a warm platter. Pour off excess fat and add pecan butter to the pan. When butter begins to foam, pour over fillets. Sprinkle with parsley and serve immediately.

*See glossary

Serves: 6
Preparation: 10 minutes
Cooking: 20 minutes

"If there is a dessert among entrées, this is it! Complete it with a crisp salad of Boston lettuce and a bottle of chablis."

BAKED STUFFED GROUPER EN CROUTE WITH SAFFRON SAUCE

—SAFFRON SAUCE—

1	large onion, coarsely chopped
1	large carrot, coarsely chopped
1	head celery, coarsely chopped
	oil or butter for sautéing
	head and bones from 2 fish, washed
5	qts. water
2	cups white wine
1	pinch saffron
2	tablespoons chopped parsley
1	stick unsalted butter
2	cups heavy cream

1. In a large (8 to 10 qt.) heavy-based pan, heat a little oil or butter. Add the onions, carrots, and celery and sauté until the vegetables are slightly softened (about 5 minutes).
2. Add the fish heads and bones. Cover the pan tightly and cook over a medium heat until the fish "sweats"* (about 10 minutes).
3. Remove the lid. Add the water, wine, and parsley and bring to a boil. Reduce the heat and simmer for 30 minutes, skimming the top often.
4. Strain the stock through a collander and then again through a fine sieve. Return to the pot and bring to a boil a second time. Boil briskly until stock is reduced to about 1 quart.
5. Lower the heat and add the butter in small pieces. Stir in the cream and the saffron, cooking until the sauce is rich and shiny. Adjust the seasoning.

—STUFFING—

8	oz. Alaskan king crab or snow crab meat, picked over for shells
8	oz. scallops
2	cups heavy cream
1	teaspoon fresh fennel

1. While the stock is reducing, combine the crab, scallops, cream and fennel in a food processor. Blend until rich and smooth (about 1 minute). Adjust the seasoning. Refrigerate for 20 minutes.

—FISH—

2	lbs. fresh grouper (4 very thin fillets, 8 oz. apiece, washed, trimmed and deboned)
1	egg, beaten
4	sheets puff pastry (10" by 7")
	oil

1. Preheat the oven to 400°F.
2. While the stuffing is chilling, prepare the fillets. Wash and trim the fish carefully of all skin and small bones. Cut into 4 equal pieces. With a sharp knife make an incision almost through each piece so that you can open the meat out like an envelope for stuffing. Or you can slice the fillets thinly so that they can be wrapped around the stuffing.
3. Put the stuffing between each piece of fish, or, if you used the second procedure, place the stuffing on top of the fillet. Close carefully, pressing gently with the fingers.
4. Lay each piece of stuffed fillet on a sheet of pastry, and carefully bring up each of the 4 sides like a small parcel, moistening each edge with beaten egg to make a firm seal.
5. Invert the parcel onto a cookie sheet brushed with oil. Brush the fish parcel with more beaten egg and make a small cut in the top to allow steam to escape.
6. Bake for 20 minutes or until pastry has risen and is golden brown.
7. To serve, pour a little of the saffron sauce on each plate and place the fish parcel carefully on the sauce. Serve the rest of the sauce at the table.

*See glossary
Serves: 4
Preparation: 30 to 45 minutes (plus 30 minutes for chilling)
Cooking: 1 hour, 20 minutes

"The chef suggests serving this dish with boiled new potatoes and fresh broccoli or asparagus. A dish fit for a king—and well worth the trouble!"

FILET OF
FISH BERMUDA

1	oz. butter
6	8-oz. portions of red snapper
1	cup dry white wine
1	cup fish stock*
2-3	shallots, minced
	salt
	white pepper
½	fresh grapefruit, peeled and diced
	diced pineapple
	grapes
	oranges, peeled and diced
	tangerines, peeled and diced
½	quart heavy cream
3	egg yolks

1. Preheat oven to 475°F.
2. Butter a pan. Arrange the fillets over the butter.
3. Add wine, stock, shallots, and salt and pepper.
4. Cover with well-buttered paper. Bake for about 12 to 20 minutes, depending upon thickness.
5. Remove fish from pan. Arrange it on a preheated platter. Cover the fish with the diced raw fruits.
6. Reduce* the juice in the pan a few minutes.
7. Whisk in the heavy cream. Stir to blend. Remove from heat.
8. Whip egg yolks and a little cream to blend. Add it to the juice and stir over a low heat for 2 minutes or until eggs are warmed through.
9. Pour it over the fish and put under broiler until golden brown.

*See glossary

Serves: 6
Preparation: 20 minutes
Cooking: 12 to 25 minutes

"We used mangrove snapper to test this recipe — delicious. The presentation at Cafe Chauveron is one of the best ever!"

19

RED SNAPPER AU PERNOD

2   lbs. snapper fillets
2   oz. butter, melted
2   shallots, finely diced
1   cup heavy cream, whipped
1   tablespoon butter
2   oz. Pernod or Anisette

1. Preheat oven to 400°F.
2. Cut the snapper into 4 equal portions.
3. Put fish into baking dish and pour melted butter on top. Bake for 15 minutes or until done.
4. In the meantime, sauté the shallots in 1 tablespoon of butter until translucent and then add the cream and Pernod. Cook for about 10 minutes or until the sauce becomes thick.
5. Serve immediately with sauce on top of the fish, surrounded by fresh green vegetables.

Serves: 4
Preparation: 5 minutes
Cooking: 20 minutes

"As you can probably tell from this cookbook there is a great affinity between fish and Pernod (or Anisette). It isn't just for coffee any more."

SAUTÉED RED SNAPPER

—FOR EACH SERVING—

5-6	oz. red snapper fillet
	salt and pepper to taste
	flour for dipping
1	beaten egg
3	tablespoons clarified butter*
	juice from ½ lemon
1	teaspoon chopped parsley
5	drops Worcestershire sauce
	lemon wedge and parsley spray
	for garnish

1. Preheat oven to 400°F.
2. Season the snapper with salt and pepper. Dip in flour, then in egg.
3. Place clear butter in hot skillet. Sauté fish for about 2 minutes on each side.
4. Place in oven and cook for 5 minutes.
5. Remove fish to warm platter.
6. Place lemon juice, parsley, and Worcestershire sauce in skillet and cook 2 to 3 minutes.
7. To serve, pour sauce over fish and garnish with lemon wedge and parsley.

*See glossary

Serves: 1
Preparation: 5 minutes
Cooking: 10 to 15 minutes

"The fillet stays moist and the flavor is delightfully piquant. Try to buy the smallest red snapper and have it filleted for you. The thin slices have the freshest, most delicate flavor."

FLORIDA
RED SNAPPER
GRECIAN

> bread crumbs
2 lbs. red snapper fillets
4 whole lemons
4 dashes of sauterne
4 oz. olive oil
1 stick butter
> sprinkle of oregano
> salt and pepper to taste

1. Preheat oven to 350°F.
2. Roll snapper fillets in bread crumbs to cover.
3. Place in a buttered oven-proof pan and baste with some of the butter and oil.
4. Place pan in oven and bake for 5 to 10 minutes, until almost cooked.
5. Take pan from oven and place under broiler to brown slightly.
6. Squeeze lemon juice over fish. Add rest of oil and butter, sauterne, oregano, and salt and pepper.
7. Place on warm serving plate and pour sauce from pan over snapper.
8. Garnish with lemon wedges and parsley. Serve immediately.

Serves: 4
Preparation: 20 minutes
Cooking: 15 to 20 minutes

"The combination of ingredients in this sauce over snapper is heavenly. Even those not too fond of fish will beg for more. Good served with pasta, buttered and creamed."

22

SNAPPER
Á L'ORANGE

This is a multi-stage recipe.

—GARNISH—

2   oranges
     water

1. Remove skin and pith from both oranges.
2. Cut the skin from one orange into julienne.*
3. Poach strips in water for 1½ minutes or until tender.
4. Remove membrane from both oranges and cut into segments. Reserve along with the julienne strips.

—WHITE WINE SAUCE—

½   stick butter, melted
¼   onion, chopped
6   oz. white wine
1½   oz. dry vermouth
1   tablespoon chopped parsley
2   cups fish stock (or clam broth)
2   tablespoons heavy cream

1. Sauté the onions in the melted butter until just soft.
2. Add white wine, vermouth, and parsley and reduce to ¾.
3. Add fish stock and let simmer 15 minutes.
4. Add heavy cream. If you are making this sauce well in advance do not add cream until just before combining with orange sauce.

—ORANGE SAUCE—

8   oz. orange juice
½   stick of butter at room
     temperature
     salt and pepper

1. Reduce* orange juice for 1 minute.
2. Take off heat and whisk in a little butter at a time until it is well incorporated.
3. Whisk in heated wine sauce and salt and pepper to taste.
4. Keep warm over a low heat or double boiler.

—FISH AND POACHING LIQUID—

½	carrot, sliced
6	oz. white wine
½	red onion, chopped
1	bay leaf
2	tablespoons chopped parsley
4	snapper fillets (6-8 oz. each), skinned

1. Combine first 5 ingredients and cook for 5 minutes.
2. Place fish in same pan and add water and/or some additional wine to cover.
3. Poach for 8 to 10 minutes or until done.
4. Remove from pan. Place on platter and top with julienne skin, orange segments and orange sauce.

Serve with rice and tomatoes that have been peeled, blanched and seeded.

*See glossary
Serves: 4
Preparation: 20 minutes
Cooking: 45 minutes

"Don't let this recipe throw you. It is easy to do in stages and much can be done in advance."

BAKED
RED SNAPPER
SPANISH STYLE

(Porgo Asado a la Espanola)

6	snapper fillets, 6-10 oz. each
1-2	medium onions, sliced ¼" thick
1-2	green peppers, sliced in ¼" thick rounds
¾	cup lemon juice mixed with 1 cup water OR ¾ cup orange juice (don't add water)
1	whole fresh garlic, peeled and pressed or mashed
1	small (14-16 oz.) can whole tomatoes in juice, crushed
	salt
	pepper
	paprika
¼	cup olive oil

1. Preheat oven to 350°F.
2. Arrange fish in pan and season with salt and pepper.
3. Place onions and peppers on top of fish.
4. Mix garlic and lemon juice together and pour over fish.
5. Sprinkle with paprika.
6. Pour on olive oil.
7. Bake 20 to 30 minutes or until fish is just done.

Serves: 6
Preparation: 15 minutes
Cooking: 20 to 30 minutes

"For garlic-lovers. Serve with rice and a green vegetable. Be sure to have some French or Italian bread to mop up the sauce. Delicious!!"

25

SNAPPER RANGOON

1	6 oz. snapper fillet
	salt and pepper to taste
	flour for dredging
1	egg
½	cup milk
5	tablespoons sweet (unsalted) butter
1½	oz. fresh lime juice
1	cup diced fruit (can use any one or a combination such as banana, melon, pineapple, strawberry, or mango)
	chopped parsley

1. Dredge fish in flour that has been mixed with salt and pepper to taste.
2. Beat egg with milk and dip fish in it.
3. Melt 2 tablespoons of butter. Sauté the fish for a few minutes and then turn over. The amount of time depends upon the thickness of the fish.
4. When fish is done, remove from heat and keep warm.
5. Melt remaining 3 tablespoons of butter. Add lime juice and fruit and cook, swirling the pan until the fruit is heated through. The juices will thicken on their own.
6. Pour the juices over the fish and sprinkle with chopped parsley.

Serves: 1
Preparation: 10 minutes
Cooking: Depends upon the size of the fish but should not take more than about 20 minutes.

"If you don't mind cleaning an extra pan, start the fruit as soon as you turn the fish over. Try to use fresh pineapple as one of the fruits. Rice with toasted almonds and a salad would be a nice accompaniment."

RED SNAPPER "ALICANTE"

½	recipe Columbia Shrimp Supreme*
2	lbs. red snapper
2	Spanish onions, sliced
4	cloves garlic, minced
½	cup olive oil
1	cup sauterne wine
¾	cup brown sauce (see glossary)
1	pinch of pepper
1	teaspoon salt
4	green peppers

—FOR GARNISH—

8	slices eggplant, breaded and fried
8	Shrimp Supreme
¼	cup sliced toasted almonds parsley

1. Make half of the Shrimp Supreme recipe.
2. Place snapper on top of onions and garlic in a casserole.
3. Over the fish, pour the olive oil, wine and brown sauce. Sprinkle with salt and a pinch of pepper, and top with green pepper slices.
4. Bake in 350°F. oven, 25 minutes or until done.

—GARNISH—

5. Garnish with eggplant, Shrimp Supreme, almonds, and parsley.

*See index

Serves: 4
Preparation: 10 minutes
Cooking: 25 to 35 minutes

"Beautiful to serve! Great tasting!"

27

FETTUCINE
WITH IRISH
SMOKED SALMON

¼	cup whipping cream
¾	lb. smoked salmon, cut julienne*
1	stick butter
¼	cup minced chives
	fresh ground pepper
1	lb. freshly cooked fettucine
	parsley sprigs to garnish

1. Combine cream and butter in medium saucepan. Cook over medium high heat until thick, glossy, and reduced by half.
2. Add salmon, chives, and pepper, and cook, stirring gently about 1 minute.
3. Transfer fettucine to serving platter. Pour sauce over and toss just to blend. Garnish with parsley and serve.

Serves: 4 to 6
Preparation: 15 minutes
Cooking: 30 minutes

*See glossary

"Leave salmon in long julienne as it tends to shrink when cooked. Do not overcook salmon. This is a good main course, served with a tossed salad and French bread. Canadian smoked salmon is a good substitute."

POTLATCH SALMON

2	lbs. king salmon cut into 4, 8-oz. steaks
1	tablespoon juniper berries
¼	cup olive oil
1½	teaspoons salt
	freshly ground black pepper
	lemon wedges
	hollandaise sauce*

1. Crush juniper berries and sprinkle them over both sides of the salmon steaks, pressing the berries into the meat so they will adhere. (Note: If you cannot find juniper berries, you can substitute ½ cup of gin. Marinate the fish in the gin for a few minutes.)
2. Coat fish with oil to prevent sticking. Sprinkle with salt and pepper.
3. Grill over hot coals, 6 minutes on each side, or pan fry in clarified butter* for approximately the same length of time.
4. Garnish with lemon wedges and serve with hollandaise sauce or any other sauce of your choice.

*See glossary

Serves: 4
Preparation: 10 minutes
Cooking: 12 minutes

"Tastes great."

MOUSSE
OF SALMON
WITH FENNEL SAUCE

1¼	pounds fillet of salmon, cut in bite size
1	cup fish stock
4	egg whites
1	cup heavy cream
¼	teaspoon salt
½	teaspoon pepper
¼	teaspoon cayenne
1	cup Fennel Sauce*

1. Preheat oven to 350°F.
2. Puree fish in an electric blender, a small amount at a time.
3. Put pureed mixture in a bowl and set bowl on ice cubes in a larger bowl. Let stand until well chilled.
4. Add fish stock gradually.
5. Add the egg whites and cream and mix to a smooth consistency.
6. Add salt, pepper and cayenne.
7. Pour into a 3-quart mold, filling it only ¾ full.
8. Place the mold in a pan half filled with hot water and bake for 15 minutes.
9. Heat Fennel Sauce in a separate pan, but do not boil.
10. When mousse is done, unmold onto a hot platter. Ladle sauce over mousse. Serve with a rice pilaf.

*See index

Serves: 6
Preparation: 5 minutes (plus Fennel Sauce and time for chilling)
Cooking: 15 minutes
"A light, flavorful concoction. Serve either as a main course or reduce the portions and use as an appetizer."

ROLLADES NORVIGIENNE

12	strips of sole fillets, 1½" wide
12	strips of Nova Scotia salmon, 1½" wide
1	cup dry white wine
¾	cup water
½	teaspoon thyme
	dash salt
	dash white pepper
1	onion, sliced
2	stalks celery, cut in large pieces
1	recipe Dill Sauce*
	lettuce leaves

1. Flatten strips of sole carefully with a flat mallet. Try to form strips of sole and salmon the same size. Place salmon on sole strips. Roll up and secure with a toothpick.
2. Bring wine, water, seasonings, onion and celery to a boil. Reduce to a simmer. Place the rollades in the simmering broth.
3. Cover the pan with foil and bake at 400°F. for 10 to 12 minutes or until fish flakes easily.
4. Drain rollades. Cool and then refrigerate.
5. To serve, trim ends to show red and white spirals. Place on lettuce leaves and cover with Dill Sauce.

*See index

Serves: 12 as a first course
Preparation: 15 minutes (plus time for chilling)
Cooking: 10 to 12 minutes

"The chef suggests a mustard sauce if you prefer it to the dill. In any case, serving extra sauce on the side is a nice touch."

SALMON CANAPES

1	8 oz. can salmon (chilled)
1	teaspoon grated onion
3	tablespoons mayonnaise
1½	teaspoons lemon juice
¼	teaspoon Worcestershire sauce
½	teaspoon paprika
¼	teaspoon salt
¼	teaspoon Tabasco sauce
12	small rounds rye bread
12	dill pickle slices

1. Drain salmon. Flake into a small bowl.
2. Add the grated onion, mayonnaise, lemon juice, Worcestershire sauce, paprika, salt and Tabasco. Taste for seasoning.
3. Spread on rye bread rounds. Top with pickle slice.

Makes: 12
Preparation: 10 minutes

"This is an easy, delicious, and cool hors d'oeuvre to make and serve."

SALMON PARISIENNE

1	salmon (4 to 5 pounds), thickly sliced
½	cup vinegar
1	large onion, sliced
1	large carrot, sliced
2	stalks celery, halved
2	bay leaves
1	teaspoon thyme
1	tablespoon salt
8	peppercorns
	parsley
1	lemon, sliced

1. Place salmon in a fish poacher or large saucepan. Add the above ingredients (with the exception of the parsley and lemon) and cover with water.
2. Slowly bring to a boiling point. If the fish is not cooked when the boiling point is reached, simmer until done. Watch carefully to make sure that you don't overcook.
3. Remove from the heat. Cool in the liquid. Remove and take off skin and any bones.
4. Place on a large platter and decorate with lemon slices and parsley.

Serve with homemade mayonnaise, tartar sauce or Russian dressing. Other appropriate sauces would be sour cream/cucumber, herbed mayonnaise or Cafe Chauveron's Fennel Sauce.* If a whole salmon is not available, salmon steaks can be used.

*See index

Serves: 6
Preparation: 5 minutes
Cooking: 20 to 25 minutes

"Leftovers make a delicious salmon salad that can be used for sandwiches or canapes. Leftover sauces can be tossed into salad greens instead of using salad dressing."

SAUMON FUMÉ
Á LA
MOUSSE DE CRABE
(Smoked Salmon Stuffed with Crab Mousse)

—STUFFING—

2	oz. snow crab meat
2	oz. Nova Scotia smoked salmon
1	oz. heavy cream
1	dash arrowroot
	dash lime juice

1. Blend the crab and salmon.
2. Dissolve the arrowroot in the cream. Add the lime juice.
3. Mix the cream mixture into the crab and salmon.

—MEDALLIONS—

1	lb. sliced smoked salmon

1. Lay the salmon, side by side, on waxed paper.
2. Place stuffing on the edge of the salmon closest to you.
3. Roll up.
4. Refrigerate until firm (30 minutes).
5. Slice diagonally and serve with green sauce.

—GREEN SAUCE—

½	cup mayonnaise
1	oz. parsley, finely chopped
1	oz. watercress, finely chopped
1	oz. spinach, finely chopped
	lemon juice
¼	tablespoon Dijon mustard

1. Blend all ingredients.
2. Refrigerate overnight before serving.

Serves: 6 to 8
Preparation: 20 minutes (plus time for chilling)

*"May be made ahead. Be sure to thoroughly cool. An
elegant appetizer."*

AMBERJACK WITH CREOLE SAUCE

6   6-oz. fillets of amberjack
lemon butter
paprika

1. Pat fillets out flat with pounder and broil in lemon butter. Sprinkle paprika on top and set aside.

—CREOLE SAUCE—

1   large onion, chopped
2   stalks celery, chopped
1   bell pepper, chopped
bacon grease
1   small can crushed tomatoes
1   small can tomato sauce
3.   teaspoons prepared roux*
2   bay leaves
pinch sweet basil
dash hot sauce
dash Worcestershire sauce
dash soy sauce
salt and pepper to taste

1. Sauté onion, celery and pepper with a little bacon grease.
2. Pour in tomatoes and tomato sauce.
3. When mixture comes to a boil, add roux to thicken.
4. Add bay leaves and boil; then add remaining seasonings and cook 10 minutes until mixture reaches gravy base consistency. Stir frequently. Serve over fish . . . or any meat, omelet or other dish.

*See glossary

Serves: 6
Preparation: 20 minutes
Cooking: 20 minutes

"Ponce de Leon himself would have feasted on this. Amberjack is a member of the salmon family."

YELLOWTAIL CALIFORNIA

2 lbs. yellowtail fillets (or other firm white fish)
Worcestershire sauce
lemon juice
salt
white pepper
flour
egg beaten with a little milk
clarified butter* for sautéing
4 slices of tomato per serving
½ small avocado per serving, cut in ¼" thick slices
bearnaise sauce
melted butter
additional lemon juice
fresh parsley, chopped

1. Preheat oven to 450°F.
2. Season the fillets in a mixture of Worcestershire, lemon juice, salt and white pepper.
3. Dip in flour, then in beaten egg.
4. Heat the clarified butter and sauté the fish on only one side.
5. Put in a buttered baking dish and pour the pan juices over the fish.
6. Top with a layer of tomato slices and then avocado.
7. Bake 8 to 10 minutes.
8. When done, remove from the heat and top with bearnaise sauce.
9. Put under broiler until just browned.
10. Top with a mixture of melted butter, lemon juice, and parsley.

*See glossary
Serves: 4
Preparation: 10 minutes
Cooking: 10 to 15 minutes

"Yellowtail is abundant in the Florida Keys but not always easy to find elsewhere. This is an elegant preparation."

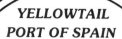

YELLOWTAIL
PORT OF SPAIN

Follow directions for seasoning, sautéing and baking Yellow-tail California.* Top with Port of Spain Sauce:

½   cup each diced bananas, apples, and pimientos
½   cup peeled, seeded, and diced tomatoes
    butter
    juice of 1 lemon
1   tablespoon chopped parsley

Simmer everything together until heated through. The apples should still be crisp. Pour on top of baked fish.

*See index

Serves: 4
Preparation: 12 minutes
Cooking: 10 to 15 minutes

"Try to catch yellowtail if you are in the Keys. It lends itself to many different preparations."

FRESH TUNA WITH LETTUCE

4	tuna steaks, 8 oz. each, and 1¼" thick
	juice of 2 lemons
4	anchovy fillets, rinsed in cold water and chopped
¼	cup olive oil
½	cup diced celery
1	Spanish onion, thinly sliced
8	large leaves of Boston lettuce, blanched in water for 2 minutes
2	tablespoons chopped dill (fresh) or 1 tablespoon dried
	salt and pepper
1⅓	cups dry white wine
½	cup chopped parsley
4	lemon wedges

1. Put steaks in a deep pan and cover with water. Squeeze lemon juice into water. Boil for 2 minutes and discard water.
2. Put onion, oil, and celery into a large saucepan and place steaks on top.
3. Slowly brown the fish steaks over a low heat.
4. When brown, turn over and arrange the anchovies and dill on top and season with salt and pepper.
5. When the fish is done, remove it from the pan and tightly wrap each steak in 2 lettuce leaves.
6. Return to the pan (covered) and gradually add the butter and the wine.
7. Simmer the fish 20 to 25 minutes or until done.
8. Put the fish in a deep serving platter and top with pan juices, vegetables, and chopped parsley. Serve lemon wedges on the side.

Serves: 4
Preparation: 20 minutes
Cooking: 25 minutes

"Fresh swordfish or salmon can be used as a replacement for the tuna. The lettuce acts as a "moisturizer" and can be served wrapped around the fish or taken off and served on the side as a tasty garnish."

38

FLORIDA SOLE
WRAPPED IN
SAVOY CABBAGE WITH CHAMPAGNE SAUCE

—FARCE—
(Stuffing)

5	lbs. fresh Florida sole, well chilled
2	oz. butter
3	oz. white bread crumbs
½	teaspoon salt
¼	teaspoon white pepper
	dash garlic powder, tarragon, basil
2½	oz. champagne
3	ice cubes

1. Combine all ingredients in a food processor or blender.
2. Blend on very high speed. Do this quickly to avoid the farce becoming warm.
3. Place in refrigerator.

—CABBAGE—

1	head savoy cabbage
2	cups white wine
½	cup water
2	cups fish bouillon (or 1 cup chicken bouillon and 1 cup water)
	farce (stuffing)

39

1. Remove 8 very large outer leaves from the cabbage.
2. Place leaves in simmering mixture of white wine and water. Blanch leaves until they are opaque and tender but firm.
3. Remove leaves. Dry each leaf on paper toweling, laying leaves flat.
4. Put wine-water mixture aside.
5. Divide farce into 8 equal portions. Place each portion on 1 leaf of cabbage, wrapping cabbage around farce in rolled form.
6. Put rolls in refrigerator and chill for 1½ to 2 hours.
7. Add fish bouillon to wine-water mixture. Bring to boil, then reduce to simmer.
8. Add the cabbage rolls and simmer 12 to 15 minutes.
9. Remove rolls. Place in warm oven on serving platter.

—CHAMPAGNE SAUCE—

1	cup fish bouillon, strained from above
½	pint heavy cream
1	oz. butter
2½	oz. champagne
2	oz. American Gold Malossal Caviar

1. Combine bouillon, heavy cream, and butter and bring to simmer.
2. Add champagne and simmer for another minute.
3. Pour champagne sauce over half of the cabbage rolls and sprinkle other half with caviar.

Serves: 4 entrées or 8 appetizers
Preparation: 45 minutes
Cooking: 30 minutes

"You can make stuffing and roll the cabbage leaves early in the day and keep refrigerated. Then, just before serving, simmer the cabbage rolls (Steps 7, 8, and 9) and make the Champagne Sauce. Magnifique!"

SOLE
IN NUT SAUCE

4	center slices of sole
3	cups Fumé de Poisson (fish stock)*
10	blanched almonds
15	hazelnuts (filberts)
2	tablespoons pine nuts (pignoli)
2	tablespoons chopped parsley
	pinch of saffron (optional)
1	small clove garlic, crushed
½	slice melba toast
	salt and white pepper
8	sprigs of dill

1. Preheat oven to 350°F.
2. Poach the sole in boiling fish stock for 3 minutes. Watch closely to make sure that it does not overcook.
3. Drain well (reserve stock) and place in an oven-proof serving dish.
4. Reserve 4 each of all the nuts for garnish. Grind the remainder with the melba toast. Mix ground nuts into the parsley, garlic, and saffron.
5. Reduce the reserved stock to 2 cups. Add nut mixture. Season to taste with salt and white pepper.
6. Pour sauce over fish and bake until sauce is heated through.
7. Garnish with dill and reserved nuts.

*See glossary

Serves: 4
Preparation: 10 minutes
Cooking: 10 to 15 minutes

"It is sometimes difficult to get hazelnuts. If that is the case substitute with half pine nuts, half almonds. If you don't have melba toast on hand, toast a thin piece of bread and then let it dry out on a rack."

FILETE
DE LENGUADO
MARBELLA
(Sautéed Fillet of Sole)

1   fillet of sole—about 6 oz.
1   banana, sliced crosswise
     clarified butter,* melted
     hollandaise sauce*

1. Preheat oven to 350°F.
2. Place sole fillet in a greased shallow pan and brush with clarified butter.
3. Arrange the banana slices over the sole.
4. Bake until done - about 10 minutes, depending upon size of fish.
5. Place on plate and cover with hollandaise sauce.
6. Serve with rice pilaf, broccoli flowerets and carrots.

*See glossary

Serves: 1
Preparation: 10 minutes
Cooking: 10 minutes

"A Spanish speciality reminiscent of Madrid!"

STUFFED POMPANO Á LA DINING GALLERIES

2	1½ lbs. pieces of pompano fillets, skinned
1	pint milk
5	oz. butter
½	oz. chopped shallots
1	clove garlic, chopped
2	oz. mushrooms, quartered
4	oz. Alaskan king crab meat
½	pint heavy cream
½	teaspoon chopped chives
	juice of 1 lemon
	pinch each of basil, tarragon, salt, white pepper
2	oz. flour
2	eggs, lightly beaten

1. Preheat oven to 350°F.
2. Soak fillets in milk for a few minutes.
3. Melt 2 oz. of butter and add shallots, garlic, and mushrooms and sauté for 30 seconds.
4. Stir in crab meat and cook until just heated through.
5. Add heavy cream and chives. Simmer until thick.
6. Season with basil, tarragon, salt, pepper, and lemon juice.
7. Remove from stove and let cool.
8. Sandwich mixture between 2 fillets. Dip in flour (shake off excess), then dip in egg.
9. Melt the remaining butter and sauté the fish until brown on both sides.
10. Put in the oven for 10 to 15 minutes.

Serves: 2
Preparation: 10 minutes
Cooking: 20 to 25 minutes

"Did you ever have such a delicious 'pompano sandwich' before? The Dining Galleries are known for their large portions!! Thank you, Chef Tevini."

POMPANO
VERONIQUE

4	pompano fillets* 1¼ lbs. each
1	teaspoon salt
	pepper to taste
4	tablespoons butter
4	shallots, chopped
3	cups dry white wine
½	cup cream sauce
4	tablespoons heavy cream, whipped
1	cup muscat grapes, seeded and skinned

*sole or any other white fish fillet can be substituted

1. Preheat broiler.
2. Season fish with salt and pepper and place in a large saucepan or fish poacher.
3. Dot with 2 tablespoons butter and sprinkle with shallots.
4. Add wine.
5. Bring to a boil and simmer slowly for 20 to 30 minutes or until fish is just done.
6. Remove fish to an oven-proof serving dish.
7. Reduce* liquid in pan until it is reduced to a third of its original quantity.
8. Work 2 tablespoons of butter into the cream sauce, then stir into liquid.
9. Correct seasoning and stir in the whipped cream.
10. Place grapes around the fish and pour the sauce over all.
11. Brown under a hot broiler.

*See glossary

Serves: 4
Preparation: 10 minutes
Cooking: 30 minutes

"Serve with spinach or broccoli and rice to help sop up the rich sauce."

MULLET
Á LA PAYSANNE

3   medium-size mullets, whole (or equivalent amount of fillets)
1   lemon, sliced
2   tablespoons butter
4   medium tomatoes, diced
2   medium green peppers, diced
½   cup sliced onions
⅓   cup olive oil
1   clove garlic, crushed
1   bay leaf
    pinch of thyme
    salt and ground black pepper to taste
½   cup dry white wine or dry vermouth
    chopped parsley for garnish

1. Preheat the oven to 350°F.
2. Clean the mullets and pat dry. Put them in a buttered baking dish.
3. Put 2 slices of lemon on top of each fillet and dot with butter.
4. Cook tomatoes, green peppers, and onions in hot olive oil in a skillet.
5. Add crushed garlic, bay leaf, thyme. Stir and cook for 5 minutes. Season to taste with salt and pepper.
6. Put the vegetable mixture around the fish. Pour the wine or vermouth over the fish and the vegetables.
7. Bake for 20 to 30 minutes (15 minutes if you use the fillets).
8. Garnish with the chopped parsley and serve.

Serves: 3
Preparation: 15 minutes
Cooking: 20 to 35 minutes

"In place of the mullet you may use other fish such as redfish, red snapper or grouper. A good, hearty, country-style way to prepare your favorite fish."

45

SMOKED MULLET
(Allow Time to Soak Ahead)

fresh whole mullet
salt
pepper
garlic
paprika

1. Remove full fillet from each side of fish. Leave skin and scales on to act as a retainer for juices.
2. Soak fillets approximately 2 hours in salt water. Remove and place on grill in smoker.
3. Season with salt, pepper, garlic, and paprika to taste.
4. Smoke with buttonwood mangrove,* if available, and cook until flaky, about 3 to 4 hours at 195°F.

*May substitute other

Serves: 1 to 2
Preparation: 2 hours to soak
Cooking: 3 to 4 hours

"Try it — you won't leave Florida without it."

SMOKED
MULLET SPREAD

2 - 3 fillets smoked mullet
½   cup chopped onion
½   cup chopped green pepper
¼   cup chopped celery
2   8-oz. pkgs. cream cheese
¼-½ cup mayonnaise
       horseradish to taste
       paprika

1. Peel fish from skin and break into small pieces. Set aside.
2. Add all ingredients to cream cheese and mix together to a smooth consistency.
3. Add smoked mullet. Form into a ball and sprinkle with paprika. Refrigerate.

Serves: 6 as an hors d'oeuvre
Preparation: 10 minutes (allow time for chilling)

"Wonderful on crackers or as a spread for a sandwich!"

FLOUNDER EN PAPILLOTE

¼	lb. butter
1	cup flour
1	qt. milk
2	tablespoons butter
1	cup finely chopped scallions
1	cup sliced mushrooms (fresh or canned)
½	teaspoon each salt and M.S.G. or Accent
1	teaspoon Worcestershire sauce
½	teaspoon Tabasco sauce
	dash of white pepper
	juice of one lemon
4	6-oz. flounder fillets
¾	cup sherry
	parchment paper
	vegetable oil
12	large cooked shrimp

1. Preheat oven to 400°F.
2. Melt butter and stir in flour to make a roux.
3. Cook and stir about 3 minutes. Gradually add milk and stir until thick.
4. Melt 2 tablespoons of butter and sauté scallions and mushrooms for 5 minutes.
5. Stir entire contents of pan into cream sauce along with the seasonings and lemon juice. Set aside to cool.
6. Steam flounder in sherry for 2 minutes.
7. Cut parchment paper into 12-inch pieces (1 per fillet).
8. Grease both sides of paper with vegetable oil.
9. Place 2 ounces of sauce in the middle of each paper and put a fillet on top. Top fillet with 3 shrimp and 3 more ounces of cream sauce. Fold paper over and twist ends.
10. Bake 10 minutes.

Serves: 4
Preparation: 15 minutes
Cooking: 15 to 20 minutes

"Serve the fillets on a dish and don't cut open until the plate is set before the lucky recipient. The aroma will delight them."

FRESH SWORDFISH GRILLÉ

	juice of 3 lemons
1½	cups olive oil
½	cup white wine
2	cloves garlic, crushed
3	tablespoons finely chopped parsley
½	teaspoon oregano
	salt and freshly ground black pepper
2	swordfish steaks, about 14 oz. each and 1" thick
	lemon wedges

1. Preheat broiler.
2. Mix lemon juice, oil, wine, garlic, parsley, oregano, salt, and pepper in a glass bowl.
3. Marinate swordfish in mixture for about 1 hour or more.
4. Drain and reserve marinade.
5. Broil fish, turning once and basting with the marinade occasionally.
6. When fish is brown cut into cubes.
7. Season with parsley and salt and pepper to taste. Mix in remaining marinade.
8. Bake in a 400°F. oven for 5 minutes. Serve with lemon wedges.

Serves: 4
Preparation: 10 minutes
Cooking: approximately 15 minutes

"The marinade helps keep the fish juicy. If you have an overabundance of shark, use that instead."

49

SAUTÉED SHAD ROE

2	pairs shad roe
	salt and freshly ground black pepper
⅓	cup flour
10	tablespoons unsalted butter
2	tablespoons Worcestershire sauce
	juice of 1 lemon
4	tablespoons chopped fresh chives
2	tablespoons chopped fresh parsley
8	crisp bacon slices (optional)

1. Cut off the skin connecting the pairs of roe.
2. Sprinkle roe with salt and pepper and dip into flour, shaking off excess flour.
3. In a large skillet melt 6 tablespoons butter over medium-high heat until butter sizzles.
4. Add roe and cook them about 5 minutes on each side or until golden brown.
5. Remove roe to a warm serving platter.
6. Add all remaining ingredients, except bacon, to the pan.
7. Bring to a quick boil. Pour over the roe. Serve roe with crisp cooked bacon, if you wish.

Serves: 4
Preparation: 5 minutes
Cooking: 15 minutes

"A delicious harbinger of spring."

STUFFED PERCH OSCAR

6 oz. shrimp, medium size
½ lb. asparagus spears
1½ lbs. thin fillets of Florida perch
½-¾ lb. crab cake
1½ cups hollandaise sauce*
Lawry's Seasoned Salt
salt and pepper
parsley for garnish

1. Clean, shell, and devein the shrimp and refrigerate.
2. Trim and wash the asparagus. Cook until almost done.
3. While the asparagus is cooking, line a shallow baking dish with half of the fillets. Spread a layer of crab cake over it. Arrange the rest of the fillets on top.
4. Bake for 15 minutes at 425°F.
5. While perch is cooking, make the hollandaise sauce and keep warm.
6. Remove the perch from the oven. Lay the asparagus spears across the top and place the shrimp between and at each end of the asparagus. Cover with the hollandaise sauce and sprinkle with Lawry's Seasoned Salt, salt and pepper.
7. Return to oven and bake for another 10 minutes.
8. When ready to serve, add some parsley for garnish.

*See glossary

Serves: 4 to 6
Preparation: 30 minutes
Cooking: 30 minutes

"This dish has so much in it that all you really need is a tossed salad and some French bread. You can purchase the crab cake as 'crab stuffing' at the fish market, or better yet, save your own and freeze when you make your own crab cakes. You can vary the proportions of perch-crab cake and add more or less hollandaise. I would vote for more sauce, just to keep the fish from drying out— plus—who wouldn't want more hollandaise?"

TED PETER'S SMOKED FISH SPREAD

2   cups finely diced onion
1   cup finely diced celery
1½   cups sweet relish with pimiento
1¼   qts. Kraft Miracle Whip
    Salad Dressing
3½   qts. flaked smoked fish
    (deboned), mullet preferred

Mix ingredients well. Chill.
Best if served in 2 to 3 days.

Serves: a party
Preparation: 10 minutes

"It's so good you could eat a whole gallon yourself."

DOLPHIN LAZARRA

1	pineapple, skinned and cored (reserve pineapple leaves)
4	medium green peppers, sliced
1	medium red onion, sliced
1	tablespoon margarine
1	teaspoon garlic salt
2	cloves garlic, minced
1½	cups crushed or stewed tomatoes
3½	lbs. dolphin (or shark or swordfish if dolphin not available)
½	teaspoon each salt and garlic powder
2	tablespoons margarine at room temperature

1. Quarter and then slice pineapple on a wooden board.
2. Remove pineapple but keep any juices that are on the board.
3. Slice the peppers and onion on the same board so that they will soak up some of the flavor of the remaining juices.
4. Melt margarine and sprinkle with garlic salt. Sauté the peppers and garlic in it until the garlic is brown. Remove with a slotted spoon.

5. Brown onions in same pan and then return the peppers, garlic, and half of the pineapple to the pan. (Try to squeeze some juice onto the vegetables.)
6. Mix salt, garlic powder, and softened margarine together and rub into fish.
7. Put fish in pan over pepper mixture and cook over a medium heat until fish has changed color halfway from the side.
8. Turn the fish over and reduce heat to low. Cook 7 minutes.
9. Fold pepper mixture over fish and add the tomatoes which have been heated.
10. Simmer for 15 minutes.
11. Serve on a tray decorated with the other half of the pineapple and the reserved pineapple leaves.

Serves: 7
Preparation: 20 minutes
Cooking: approximately 30 to 40 minutes

"Co-owner Steve Knight improvised this dish on the spur of the moment and named it after his partner, Bob Lazzara. Try this inspiration!"

BLACK SEA BASS ST. AUGUSTINE

—FILLING—

1	oz. chopped shallots
2	oz. chopped scallions
4	oz. butter
4	oz. flour
½	cup light cream
½	lb. king crab meat, chopped
1	oz. wine
	salt to taste
	pepper to taste
	lemon juice to taste
1	cup bread crumbs
2	medium eggs, whipped lightly with a fork

1. Sauté the shallots and scallions in the butter until tender. Whisk in the flour and stir constantly to make a roux. Simmer 5 to 10 minutes.
2. Add the cream and heat just to boiling. Lower heat and simmer, stirring to make smooth.
3. Add the crab meat, wine, salt, pepper, and lemon juice. Taste and adjust the seasonings. Remove from heat.
4. Add the bread crumbs and the eggs and mix well. The filling should be stiff but spreadable. Chill.

—BASS—

2 - 4 lb. black sea bass fillets
¼ cup lemon juice
flour as needed
egg as needed
clarified butter* as needed
hollandaise sauce*

1. Preheat oven to 350°F.
2. Flatten the bass and marinate in the lemon juice for 15 minutes.
3. Spread the fillets with the filling and roll up. Tie if necessary.
4. Dredge each rolled fillet in flour and dip in the lightly beaten egg.
5. Sauté the fillets in the butter until golden.
6. Bake for 20 to 25 minutes. Let rest 10 to 15 minutes before serving. Pour the hollandaise sauce over the fillets.

*See glossary

Serves: 6
Preparation: 40 minutes
Cooking: 40 minutes

"The chef suggests serving this attractive dish with snow peas and stuffed new potatoes."

SMOKED FISH DIP

1   lb. smoked fish (kingfish, marlin,
    tuna or sailfish)
1   stalk of celery
¼   onion
    Tabasco sauce
    mayonnaise
    lime juice

1. Grind smoked fish, celery and onion into a mixing bowl, using the paddle of the mixer. Blend at a slow speed.
2. Add enough mayonnaise to bind.
3. Season with Tabasco and lime juice.

Serves: 6 to 10 as an hors d'oeuvre
Preparation: 5 minutes

"Serve with crackers. You'll want to move to the Keys right away."

Notes

BOSS
BASS

Fresh Water Fin Fish

Florida is often thought of as a fishing paradise. In addition to an almost endless variety of salt water fish, fresh water are abundant in lakes, rivers, creeks, marshes, and even ditches where some bass have been caught. Before you grab your pole and go flying off, be aware that there are definite "seasons" for fresh water fish; some even as short as three days. So be absolutely, positively sure that you have a permit or license if one is necessary. People have been known to be arrested and/or fined for illegal catches.

All You Ever Wanted To Know ...

When we started researching this book, we found that there are hundreds of theories about how to catch fish and what to use to catch them. (See the References Section for suggested books.) There are also clubs that teach how to catch trout, once thought of as a rich man's sport. In general going after large fresh water fish is less expensive than going after salt water game fish. After all you can catch large bass just by wading into a lake; no chartering or owning a deep sea boat.

"Handle With Care"

Most experts* suggest that (1) when you catch most fresh water fish you should keep them in a well-ventilated creel in layers separated by dry grasses; (2) kill and draw trout as quickly as possible; (3) don't wash your cleaned catch until just ready to cook as the flesh is weakened and deteriorates quickly.

See the salt water section on information on how to buy, etc.

*Tom Cofield in his book **The Fisherman's Guide to North America**, points out that often the difference between an expert and a novice is the amount of publicity given to an expert's accomplishments and lack of publicity when no fish are caught.

Fresh Water Fin Fish and Their Fat Content

FAT
6 to 20% or more

Chub   Smelt
Pike (Northern, Blue)   Yellow Perch

INTERMEDIATE
2 to 6%

Alewife   Carp
Bass (small)   Catfish
Bass (large)   Drum (fresh water)
Brook Trout   Pickerel
Buffalo Fish   Sucker

LEAN
Less than 2%

Bullhead (black)   Rainbow Trout
Crappie   Salmon
Lake Trout   Shad
Mullet (striped)   Whitefish (lake)
Perch

CATFISH

4   catfish fillets, cut in 2-3" strips
     salt and pepper to taste
     Accent (same amount as salt)
     dash paprika
1   cup cornmeal, stone ground*
     oil for frying

1. Lightly season cornmeal with salt, pepper and Accent. Add a little paprika for coloring.
2. Dip catfish strips in meal mixture and deep fry until golden brown. Fish gets cooked evenly throughout.

Hint: Sift the used cornmeal to get rid of lumps from the dampness of the fish each time you make this recipe. Store meal in refrigerator and re-use.

Serves: 2 to 4
Preparation: 10 minutes
Cooking: 5 to 10 minutes

*"Chef Steve Johnson insists on using only fresh, stone-ground cornmeal made by old-time Georgia Crackers who live in the woods near Atlanta. Their meal looks like real fine face powder, he says, and is also good for making grits. If you want to make 'the real McCoy,' write to Steve and he'll provide details on ordering."

BONELESS
STUFFED TROUT
"PETER'S PLACE"

½ stick butter
½ cup sliced mushrooms
½ cup baby shrimp, well rinsed
2 teaspoons chopped chives
½ cup chopped sweet onion
  dash white pepper and salt
1 teaspoon chopped green pepper
1 teaspoon Anisette or Pernod
  juice of ½ lemon
2 boneless brook or rainbow trout
  olive oil

1. Melt ¼ stick butter and sauté mushrooms until browned and soft.
2. Melt other ¼ stick of butter and sauté the shrimp, chives, and onion until onions are golden and the mixture is hot Add Anisette, parsley, pepper, and salt.
3. Stuff the trout with the hot mixture.
4. Sprinkle with lemon juice and truss the trout with toothpicks.
5. Using your hands, rub olive oil all over the trout.
6. The trout can be cooked the following ways immediately after stuffing: on an open grill, broiled or sautéed. In any case, figure 3 minutes per side or just until the flesh becomes white.

Serves: 2
Preparation: 15 minutes
Cooking: 6 minutes

"If fresh baby shrimp are not available, use canned shrimp or small shrimp sliced and cut in small pieces. If you are going to grill the trout, lightly brush the grill with olive oil to prevent sticking. Finely chopped scallions can be used as a substitute for chives in a pinch."

TROUTE MEUNIERE

1	freshwater trout, cleaned and boned
	garlic salt
	salt and pepper
	flour
2	tablespoons butter, melted
1	teaspoon finely chopped shallot
1	teaspoon lemon juice
	dry sherry
	parsley, lemon slices, watercress

1. Sprinkle trout with garlic salt about 1 hour before cooking.
2. Season with salt and pepper. Dip in flour and shake off excess.
3. Melt butter over a high heat. Cook trout until both sides are brown and the flesh is cooked. Transfer to a platter.
4. Add a little more butter to the same pan. Sauté the shallot until translucent and add lemon juice and a generous splash of sherry.
5. Deglaze* pan and pour remaining juices over trout.
6. Garnish with parsley, lemon, and watercress.

*See glossary

Serves: 1
Preparation: 5 minutes
Cooking: about 10 minutes

"An easy recipe that can be done 'by the stream' if you bring along the necessary ingredients."

TRUITE BRAISEE AU CHAMPAGNE

(Trout Braised in Champagne)

1	shallot, chopped
1	onion, chopped
2	carrots, julienne*
2	celery stalks, julienne*
¼	lb. butter
1	2-lb. fresh trout boned, or 4 trout, boned (10 oz. each)
4	slices bacon
1	head of lettuce, leaves separated
	salt and pepper
2	cups champagne
2	tablespoons heavy cream

1. Preheat oven to 400°F.
2. Melt butter and simmer the shallot, onion, carrots, and celery for 5 minutes.
3. Remove vegetables with a slotted spoon and reserve the melted butter.
4. Stuff the trout with the vegetables.
5. Wrap bacon slices around the trout and then wrap in the lettuce leaves.
6. Put trout into an oven-proof baking dish and brush with the reserved butter.
7. Sprinkle with salt and pepper and pour champagne over all.
8. Bake for 20 minutes. Remove from oven and take off the bacon and lettuce.
9. Add the cream and return to the oven for 2 minutes or until the cream has heated through.

*See glossary

Serves: 4
Preparation: 15 minutes
Cooking: 25 minutes

"If you cannot get whole trout, use fillets. Stuff and roll up each fillet and proceed as directed."

TROTA ALLA PRIMAVERA
(Trout Primavera)

¼ lb. butter
2 carrots, julienne*
1 zucchini, julienne
handful of snow pea pods, julienne
1 green pepper, julienne
1 can pimientos, julienne
1 small onion, julienne
2 celery stalks, julienne
2 fresh trout fillets, 12-14 oz. each
milk for dipping
flour
2 tablespoons fresh basil or
½ teaspoon dry (optional)
salt and pepper to taste
2 cups hollandaise sauce*
1 cup whipping cream

1. Melt butter in large skillet. Add vegetables in order of cooking time (i.e., carrots first). Sauté until cooked but still crunchy (5 minutes). Season with basil, salt and pepper and put aside.
2. Dip fish fillets in milk. Dust with flour and sauté on both sides. Place in baking dish. Top with vegetables. (May be prepared 1 day in advance at this point and refrigerated.)
3. Mix hollandaise with whipping cream. Keep warm.
4. Heat trout and vegetables in 325°F. oven. Serve with hollandaise-cream mixture over top.

*See glossary

Serves: 2 to 3
Preparation: 15 minutes
Cooking: 15 minutes

"A beautiful dish. You'll love the decor at the famous Casa Vecchia."

BOILED
SHRIMP

Shrimp

These gregarious, tender, delicate, and delicious little creatures are the most popular shellfish eaten in the United States. And it's no wonder when you consider their outstanding flavor, ease of preparation, health-giving goodness, low caloric count, eye appeal, their ability to be combined with many other ingredients, plus their availability and versatility. And, they've been "on the menu" since the time of Confucius who had words of praise for them.

Rich, Rich, Rich

Shrimp are very high in nutrition. At only 35 calories per ounce, they contain large amounts of lean protein, vitamins A, B, and D, and are rich in minerals.

In Florida, the three commercially important shrimp are white, brown, and pink. No matter what the original color, when cooked the shells turn pink, the meat is white, and the flavor and nutritional values are the same.

Versatility Plus

Shrimp lend themselves to a multitude of cooking styles: they can be sautéed, simmered, broiled, barbequed, battered and deep fried, stuffed, added to sauces, soups or salads, or used as a garnish for other fish dishes. They can be made into a paste or turned into croquettes.

A "Hotbed" Of Shrimp

The largest shrimp fishery in the world is the Gulf of Mexico. Several hundred million pounds are taken annually by the shrimpers in the United States, Mexico, and Cuba. Commercially, shrimp are caught with hand or cast nets, baited traps, haul seines, and the most frequently used boat-drawn beam and otter trawls. Trawlers, dragging their large, bag-like nets, are often seen out on the Gulf.

How To Catch

If you happen to be in southern Florida and feel like catching them yourself, you can try it—from a seawall, a boat, or from a dock. Wait until dark, and go out with your lantern and a long, finely meshed scoop net. If there are shrimp in the neighborhood, they will be attracted to the light, and you can scoop them up with your net. You don't need a permit, but the State of Florida says they should be no smaller than 45 shrimp (with their heads on) to a pound.

Buying Shrimp

Shrimp can be purchased fresh (known as "green" shrimp), frozen, canned, or dried. They are available all year round, but they're always cheaper in season, November through April.

If you are buying them fresh, look for shrimp that are firm in texture and have a mild odor with no iodine smell. They should be almost translucent, with no discoloration. If they still have their heads, make sure they are attached firmly to the bodies. They should be cooked within one or two days of purchase. If you are not going to cook them until later, it would be best to freeze them immediately after purchase. Cooked shrimp can be stored in the refrigerator for up to three days.

If you are buying frozen shrimp, make sure they are solidly frozen, have little or no odor, no brown spots, and no sign of freezer burn (indicated by a very white, dry appearance around the edges).

How To Freeze

Wash the shrimp well, rinse several times, and seal in bags. If you are planning to store them for a long time, remove the heads. Frozen shrimp maintain their flavor for up to six months. It is preferable to freeze only raw shrimp. When you are ready to cook them, simply add them to whatever dish you are making; there is no need to defrost before cooking.

Sizes Of Shrimp

Size	Raw Shrimp In Shell From One Pound
Jumbo	up to 15
Large	16 to 18
Medium	26 to 30
Small	60 or more

Because there is a lot of shrinkage in cooking and shelling, a good rule of thumb is that two pounds of raw, headless, unpeeled shrimp nets about one pound cooked.

How To Shell And Devein

Hold tail of raw or cooked shrimp in your left hand. Slip thumb of right hand under the shell at the large end of the shrimp between the feelers and lift off two or three segments of shell. Gently ease shrimp out of shell. Then, make a shallow cut lengthwise along the back to expose the sand vein, a black thread-like part. Holding it under running water, remove it with your fingers, a knife tip, or a toothpick. Rinse.

Cooking

There is one rule for all shrimp: *never overcook.* If they are fresh, drop them into boiling stock or water. Reduce the heat at once and simmer 3 to 4 minutes. Remove them before they start to curl. Drain. Shrimp may be cooked before or after shelling and deveining; however, cooking with the shells imparts a better flavor.

Save the shells. You can grind them in a food processor to make a shrimp butter to be used as a flavoring for other sauces to be poured over poached fish.

Rock Shrimp

A note should be made here about the lesser known rock shrimp. A Florida native, this succulent delight with a taste that hovers between lobster and shrimp, is very perishable. Therefore, most rock shrimp are marketed in the raw, frozen state as either whole or split tails. The largest size they come in is usually 21 to 25 per pound. Like shrimp, they can lose half their weight after being cooked and shelled. They can be used in most any recipe calling for shrimp. However, they cook in *less time* than do shrimp, so proceed accordingly.

70

SHRIMP ROCKEFELLER

—BOILED SHRIMP—

4   lbs. shrimp, fresh or frozen (20 per lb. size)
    pinch of each - salt, white pepper, cayenne pepper
1   lemon cut in half

1. Be sure shrimp are thoroughly thawed. Place in pot and cover with cold water.
2. Add salt, pepper, and both pieces of lemon, and heat only to a boil.
3. Immediately pour through a collander.
4. Run cold water over the shrimp and peel and devein them while warm.
5. Set aside.

—SPINACH BASE—

1   lb. frozen spinach, thawed and cut into 1" squares
6   green onions, trimmed and chopped
1   bunch parsley, chopped fine
1   bunch celery, chopped medium
1   garlic clove, chopped
1   tablespoon salt
1   teaspoon white pepper
1   drop Tabasco sauce
3   tablespoons Worcestershire sauce
½   lb. butter

1. Melt butter in heavy-bottomed pot.
2. Add drained spinach and simmer for 10 minutes.
3. Add all remaining ingredients, including spices, and simmer for about 1 hour, uncovered, stirring occasionally. Be sure that celery is cooked enough so that it is not crisp.
4. Set aside.

71

—MORNAY SAUCE—

½	lb. butter
¾	cup flour
1	qt. milk (heated to boiling point)
1	lb. Swiss or Gruyere cheese, grated
	pinch cayenne pepper
1	teaspoon white pepper
3	oz. grated Parmesan cheese

1. Preheat oven to 425°F.
2. Melt butter and blend in flour over the heat. While you are blending in the flour, make sure the milk is very hot without boiling.
3. Take pot containing blended flour and butter (roux) off the heat and add the milk. Stir vigorously with a wire whip until roux is thickened.
4. Place the pot back on high heat and continue stirring. As sauce thickens add salt, pepper, cayenne pepper and grated cheese.
5. Allow the sauce to come to a boil momentarily. Taste and adjust seasoning if necessary. Remove from heat immediately and pour into another container.
6. Cover the bottom of a 2 to 3-quart casserole with the spinach mixture.
7. Lay all the shrimp over the spinach.
8. Ladle the sauce over the shrimp and then sprinkle with grated Parmesan cheese, melted butter, and paprika.
9. Bake for 20 minutes.

Serves: 8
Preparation: 30 minutes
Cooking: 1½ hours

"The shrimp and spinach base can be made earlier in the day and refrigerated — A richly Rockefeller dish!"

GARLIC SHRIMP

shrimp - the largest you can find,
frozen or fresh
melted butter or margarine or
Parkay Liquid Margarine
Lawry's Seasoned Garlic Salt

1. Shell and devein the shrimp and arrange on an aluminum platter.
2. Cover with melted butter or margarine and sprinkle with seasoned garlic salt.
3. Put under the broiler for a couple of minutes. Turn and broil on the other side. When shrimp is pink, it is ready to eat, so watch the shrimp closely so as not to overcook.

Serves: depends upon the amount of shrimp you cook
Preparation: ditto
Cooking: 5 to 6 minutes

"Easy and so tasty . . . No matter how many shrimp you make, and no matter how many people there are . . . the shrimp will disappear! Another version of this is beer shrimp: instead of butter and garlic salt, use beer, salt and pepper and prepare as above."

PASTA DI MEDICI

1	lb. fusili pasta, cooked al dente* (available at gourmet specialty shops)
10	fresh jumbo shrimp (10-15 per lb.), cooked and sliced in half
2	oz. fresh chopped basil
2	oz. fresh rosemary
2	oz. fresh chopped chives
2	oz. scallions cut on bias (julienne)*
2	oz. zucchini cut on bias (julienne)*
2	oz. Westphalian ham (julienne)*
2	oz. shallots, chopped
2	oz. garlic, chopped
	fresh grated Parmesan cheese to taste
1	cup olive oil
¼	cup lemon juice
¼	cup red wine vinegar

1. Combine all ingredients in a bowl and toss lightly.

*See glossary

Serves: 4 to 6
Preparation: 15 minutes
Cooking: 10 minutes

"Wonderful spices and herbs combine to make this tutto bene!"

SHRIMP MERLIN

3	lbs. large raw shrimp, shelled and deveined
3	quarts water
1	tablespoon thyme
½	teaspoon basil
4	hard-cooked egg yolks
4	tablespoons white wine vinegar
2-3	tablespoons sugar or more to taste
1	teaspoon dry mustard
¼	teaspoon black pepper
2½	cups mayonnaise
4	oz. capers
2	medium onions, thinly sliced
½	cup whipped cream
½	cup sour cream (whipped until smooth)
	lettuce for garnish

1. Bring water to boil in a large pot. Add thyme, basil, and shrimp.
2. Bring to boil again, reduce heat and simmer for 5 minutes or until just done and shrimp is pink. Drain and cool completely.
3. Press 4 egg yolks through sieve into a large bowl. Add vinegar, sugar, mustard, pepper and mayonnaise. Blend well.
4. Add capers, onions and shrimp. Blend well again.
5. Fold in whipped cream and sour cream. Taste for seasoning. You may wish to add more pepper and a dash of salt.
6. To serve, place in lettuce cups and garnish as you wish.

Serves: 6 to 8 as entrée, salad or first course
Preparation: 25 minutes (plus time for chilling)
Cooking: 5 minutes

"We found the divergent sweet and sour taste intriguing. Could be garnished with cherry tomatoes and chopped parsley or fruits."

SHRIMP LOUIS

—FOR EACH SERVING—

1	cup fresh or frozen shrimp (70-90 per lb. size)
3-4	leaves leaf lettuce
1	cup shredded iceberg lettuce
½	tomato, quartered
1	hard-boiled egg
3-4	pitted black olives
½	cup chick peas
1	green pepper ring
	dressing

1. On platter, place 3 or 4 leaves of leaf lettuce. Cover center of platter with shredded iceberg.
2. Top with shrimp.
3. Garnish rest of dish with the remaining ingredients.
4. Top with Shrimp Louis Dressing.

SHRIMP LOUIS DRESSING

1	cup mayonnaise
1½	cup chili sauce
¼	green pepper, chopped
1-2	tablespoons chopped pimiento
	paprika
	salt and pepper to taste
¼	teaspoon dry mustard
1	tablespoon chopped onion
	dash Tabasco sauce
¼	teaspoon horseradish

1. Mix above ingredients together.
2. Chill thoroughly. Makes 2½ cups - enough for 2 to 4 servings.

Preparation: 25 minutes

"Shrimp Louis is served at Joe's only at lunch. It's a most refreshing salad with a great distinctive flavor."

SHRIMP
SUZANNE WITH DILL

1	lb. (25-30 count) shrimp, cooked, peeled, and cleaned
½	cup sour cream
½	cup mayonnaise
½	cup cucumber soup or ½ fresh cucumber, seeded and scraped with spoon
⅓	cup finely chopped onions
1½	tablespoons fresh chopped dill
1½	teaspoons lemon juice
½	teaspoon garlic salt
¼	teaspoon fresh ground pepper
¼	teaspoon or 8 drops Tabasco sauce
¼	teaspoon caraway seed

1. Mix ingredients well. Chill well.
2. Serve on a bed of Bibb lettuce, either as individual servings or in lettuce-lined bowls.

Serves: 4 to 6
Preparation: 15 minutes

"Refreshing and delicious!"

SHRIMP MOUSSE

2	egg whites
2	cups heavy cream
1½	teaspoons salt
½	teaspoon white pepper
¼	teaspoon nutmeg
1	lb. shrimp—raw, shelled, deveined
	Shrimp Sauce*

1. Preheat oven to 350°F.
2. Combine egg whites, heavy cream, and seasonings in a small bowl.
3. Pour one third of mixture into a blender or food processor. Add one third of the shrimp. Blend into the consistency of a smooth paste, scraping the sides once or twice. Pour into a large mixing bowl. Repeat process until all ingredients are used. Mix well.
4. Pour into a fancy 1-quart mold. A fish shape would be perfect.
5. Place mold in a pan of water. Cover with aluminum foil and bake for about 40 minutes.
6. Remove from oven and allow to rest for 5 minutes. Loosen edges; turn out onto serving platter and cover with Shrimp Sauce.

*See index

Serves: 4 to 6
Preparation: 30 minutes
Cooking: 40 minutes

"This is a very rich dish, perfect for a first course. As a main course, serve with garden salad with not too pungent a dressing to overpower the delicate shrimp flavor of the mousse. Dish may 'rest' for awhile, keeping warm, while you prepare the rest of the meal."

SCAMPI AMERICANA

2½ lbs. jumbo shrimp (6-8 shrimp per lb.), peeled and deveined, shells reserved
flour
3 tablespoons chopped scallions
1 tablespoon capers
3 oz. clarified butter*
2 oz. white wine
juice of 1 lemon
4 oz. reduced* shrimp stock made from water and reserved shells
2 oz. light brown veal sauce*
3 oz. garlic butter*
salt and pepper

1. Butterfly* the shrimp.
2. Melt the butter in a large skillet. Dust the shrimp with flour and sauté until light brown.
3. Add scallions and capers, and sauté for 1 minute. Add white wine, lemon juice, shrimp stock and brown sauce— let simmer.
4. Put shrimp over rice pilaf (see index).
5. Reduce sauce in pan until somewhat thick. Season with salt and pepper to taste.
6. Whisk in the garlic butter and pour over shrimp.

*See glossary
Serves: 4
Preparation: 20 minutes
Cooking: 10 minutes

"This is super easy and quick if you have the brown sauce on hand."

BAKED SCAMPI

½	lb. butter
2	tablespoons Grey Poupon Mustard
1	tablespoon lemon juice
1	tablespoon chopped garlic
1	tablespoon chopped parsley
2	lbs. raw shrimp (21 to 25 per pound), peeled, leaving the shell on the tail

1. Combine all the ingredients except the shrimp in a small saucepan, and heat over low heat for about 10 minutes.
2. Arrange shrimp in a shallow baking dish. Pour butter mixture over shrimp.
3. Bake at 450°F. for about 12 to 15 minutes, or until the shrimp lose their translucent look.
4. Garnish with parsley and lemon wedges.

Serves: 6
Preparation: 30 minutes—includes shelling
Cooking: 25 minutes

"Easy to make and so classic!"

SCAMPI PROVENCALE

⅛	cup butter
3	cloves garlic, minced
30	medium to large shrimp, peeled and sliced lengthwise
2	cups sliced mushrooms
½	cup thinly sliced zucchini
5	tomatoes, peeled and diced
	approximately 1 cup white wine

1. Lightly sauté the garlic in the butter.
2. Add shrimp and sauté until half way cooked.
3. Add mushrooms and zucchini and sauté 2 minutes.
4. Add tomatoes. When ingredients are tender, add wine and simmer 2 minutes.
5. Serve over your favorite rice recipe.

Serves: 6
Preparation: 20 minutes
Cooking: 10 minutes

"An elegant touch would be to serve this dish with a combination of white and wild rice. Taste this and you're in the south of France!"

SHRIMP SCAMPI RAINTREE

1	lb. sweet butter, well chilled and cut in large slices
4	cloves garlic
2	tablespoons chopped parsley oil for sautéing
1	lb. mushrooms, quartered
1½	lbs. jumbo shrimp, peeled and deveined
1	cup white wine
1	tablespoon lemon juice
2	oz. Parmesan cheese
1	pint heavy cream
1	lb. cooked buttered noodles

1. In a food processor: combine butter, garlic, and parsley and blend until smooth (about 1 minute).
2. Heat oil in a large skillet. Add mushrooms and swirl them in the oil. Add shrimp and cook over high heat for 30 seconds, stirring constantly.
3. Reduce heat slightly, pour off excess oil (leave a slight film of oil in the pan).
4. Add wine, lemon juice, Parmesan, and cream. Continue cooking for about 1 minute or until the cream has reduced slightly.
5. Add butter-garlic-parsley combination.
6. Reduce heat a little more and continue cooking for 3 or 4 minutes until the butter is incorporated and the sauce has a shiny appearance.
7. Serve over the hot noodles.

Serves: 4
Preparation: 15 minutes
Cooking: 10 minutes (plus the noodles—or start cooking the noodles right after starting the mushrooms)

"This is an easy and excellent recipe. Serve with asparagus or broccoli and a sliced tomato salad for a good interplay of taste and texture."

SHRIMP GENOVESE

2	lbs. large raw shrimp, shelled and deveined

—MARINADE—

2	cups olive oil
½	cup red wine vinegar
1	cup white wine (Rhine or sauterne suggested)
3	cloves garlic, mashed
1	teaspoon basil (fresh is nice if available)
¼	teaspoon thyme
1	bay leaf, broken into pieces
1	clove, bruised
1	teaspoon onion powder
1	lemon, juiced and cut in pieces

1. Mix all marinade ingredients. Blend well.
2. Add shrimp and marinate 3 to 4 hours.
3. Drain shrimp and broil 2 or 3 minutes. Do not overcook. Marinade cooks the shrimp slightly.

Serves: 6 to 8 as appetizer
Preparation: 15 minutes (plus time for marinating)
Cooking: 2 to 3 minutes

"Delicious appetizer. You can add a little chopped red pepper if you like."

COCONUT SHRIMP

5   shrimp (16-20 to a lb.), shelled and deveined
½   cup flour
¾   cup milk
2   eggs, slightly beaten
3½ oz. shredded coconut
    Coconut Amaretto liqueur
    pineapple rings
    Mustard Fruit Sauce (see index)

1. Butterfly shrimp.*
2. Dust shrimp in flour.
3. Dip floured shrimp in egg/milk combination.
4. Roll shrimp in shredded coconut.
5. Deep fry until golden brown.
6. Sprinkle with coconut. Lightly sprinkle with Coconut Amaretto.
7. Garnish plate with pineapple rings. Serve with a soufflé cup of warmed Mustard Fruit Sauce.

*See glossary

Serves: 1
Preparation: 5 minutes
Cooking: 2 to 4 minutes

"The chef serves this in the tradition of the Hana-Maui in Hawaii; with a tangy mustard fruit sauce, using the famous mustard fruits from Cremona, Italy, pineapple garnish and your choice of potato."

COLUMBIA
SHRIMP SUPREME

16	jumbo shrimps, peeled and deveined, and tail left on
	juice of one lemon
1	teaspoon garlic powder
½	teaspoon pepper
1	teaspoon salt
8	strips of bacon
2	eggs, lightly beaten
½	cup of milk
	flour

1. Pat shrimp dry. Marinate in lemon juice, garlic, salt and pepper for 10 minutes.
2. Cut bacon strips in half, wrap around shrimp and secure with a toothpick.
3. Beat together egg and milk and dip shrimp in batter. Roll in flour.
4. Deep fry at 300°F. until golden brown (about 5 to 8 minutes).

Serves: 2 as a main course
Preparation: 15 minutes
Cooking: 5 minutes

"You can't eat just one."

SHRIMP CREOLE

½	cup chopped celery
½	cup chopped onion
¼	cup chopped salt pork
1	2½ lb. can tomatoes
6	oz. chili sauce
2	oz. tomato paste
½	teaspoon thyme
1	teaspoon Maggi seasoning
2	cloves garlic, finely chopped
	salt and pepper
2	lbs. shrimp, peeled, deveined and cooked

1. Simmer celery, onions and salt pork until salt pork is cooked.
2. Add all the other ingredients (except shrimp) and cook for 30 minutes over a low flame.
3. Add shrimp and warm through.
4. Serve over rice.

Serves: 4 to 6
Preparation: 15 minutes
Cooking: 45 minutes

"This is a Floridian version of creole that is quite good. And you thought that Joe's had only great stone crabs!"

SHRIMP CURRY

—CURRY SAUCE—

3	oz. clarified butter*
4	cloves garlic, chopped
3	ribs celery, chopped
1	large carrot, chopped
2	medium onions, chopped
1	bunch parsley, chopped
2	oz. good curry powder
1¾	qts. chicken velouté sauce*
4	oz. white wine
2	medium tomatoes, peeled, seeded, and chopped
	juice and rind of 2 large oranges
½	teaspoon each of mace, cloves, cayenne, coriander, ginger, and white pepper
¾	teaspoon each of cinnamon and allspice
12	oz. heavy cream
	salt

1. Gently sauté garlic, celery, carrot, and onion in 3 ounces of clarified butter for 5 minutes.
2. Add parsley and curry powder. When powder turns light brown, add the white wine and chicken velouté sauce.
3. Simmer for 5 minutes and then add the next 12 ingredients.
4. Simmer for 30 to 45 minutes, strain, and add salt to taste.

—SHRIMP—

6	oz. clarified butter
3	lbs. jumbo shrimp, peeled and deveined
3	Red Delicious apples, peeled, cored, and cut into julienne*
12	oz. mango chutney
6	hard-cooked egg yolks, grated
1	cup currants
1	cup toasted coconut, shredded

1. Butterfly* the shrimp and sauté in 6 ounces of hot clarified butter. When shrimp just begin to cook, add the curry sauce and simmer for 5 minutes.
2. Add apples and remove from heat.
3. Serve on timbales of rice pilaf and accompany with chutney, yolks, currants, and toasted coconut.

—RICE PILAF—

2	cups rice
4	cups well-seasoned chicken stock
1	small onion, diced
2	bay leaves
1	rib celery, diced
2	oz. butter

1. Sauté the onion and celery rib in 2 ounces of butter.
2. When onion turns golden, stir in the rice, making sure that it is well coated with the butter.
3. Add chicken stock and bring to boil.
4. Add bay leaves and simmer 20 to 25 minutes until done.

*See glossary

Serves: 6
Preparation: 30 minutes
Cooking: approximately 45 minutes (not including rice)

"A favorite of Park Plaza Gardens' customers!"

SHRIMP LAUREN

1½	lbs. large shrimp or scallops, cooked
½	cup butter
½	cup olive oil
	salt and pepper
1	oz. fresh garlic (3 to 4 cloves), slightly mashed
1	lb. celery, peeled and coarsely chopped
½	lb. onion, minced
1	lb. green pepper cut in ¾ inch squares (use some red pepper for color if desired)
¼	cup lemon juice
1	lb. tomatoes, coarsely chopped

1. In a large heavy skillet melt butter. Add olive oil, salt, and pepper. Add garlic and sauté garlic until soft.
2. Add celery. Cook covered until celery softens. Add onion and peppers. Cook, stirring frequently until vegetables are nearly done and still crunchy.
3. Stir in lemon juice and remove from heat.
4. Add tomatoes after contents of pan cool somewhat. Cover for few minutes and continue to cool.
5. If serving immediately, add the shellfish, mix well and serve. Garnish with parsley.

NOTE:
If preparing ahead, let cool and store until serving time. At TIME OF SERVICE put into individual casseroles or large casserole. Add prepared shellfish and place in oven until hot. Serve.

Serves: 6 to 8
Preparation: 15 minutes
Cooking: 15 minutes

"This is a great dish if you are trying to save on calories or just love shrimp. The fresh ingredients make a beautiful presentation."

SHRIMP CURACAO

1	orange, squeezed and peel reserved
1	cup hollandaise sauce*
12	large raw shrimp, peeled and deveined
	salt and pepper to taste
3	oz. clarified butter*
2	oz. orange Curaçao (Do not substitute lower proof liqueur, it will not flame.)
2	cups wild rice pilaf (prepared as you wish)
½	cup whipped cream
1	bunch watercress for garnish

1. Cut zest from orange into very fine julienne.* Blanch and cool.
2. Prepare hollandaise sauce and add juice from orange. Keep warm.
3. Season shrimp with salt and pepper.
4. Heat butter in large heavy skillet. Sauté shrimp 2 to 3 minutes or until just tender.
5. Flambé* with warmed Curaçao.
6. Reduce cooking liquid in pan about 2 minutes. Do not overcook shrimp.
7. To serve, arrange shrimp in a line over 2 individual servings of rice. Nap with orange hollandaise. Top with a dollop of whipped cream, sprinkle with orange julienne and garnish with watercress.

*See glossary

Serves: 2
Preparation: 30 to 35 minutes
Cooking: 6 minutes, plus time for hollandaise sauce and rice.

"Lovely looking and delicious tasting. An unusual way to prepare shrimp."

HAWAIIAN SHRIMP WITH SHERRY SAUCE

—SHRIMP—

1   lb. of large shrimp (or 10 shrimp), shelled and deveined—reserving shells
    garlic salt to taste
    juice of ½ lemon
10 small slices of fresh or canned pineapple
1   green pepper, cut into 10 strips
5   slices of bacon, cut in half and blanched*
3   oz. pineapple juice
3-4 tablespoons melted butter

1. Marinate shrimp in garlic salt and lemon juice for 10 minutes.
2. Wrap a shrimp, a pineapple slice, and a green pepper strip with a strip of bacon. Secure with toothpick. Pour over pineapple juice. Marinate one hour in refrigerator.

*See glossary

THE LOBSTER POT—REDINGTON SHORES

—SHERRY SAUCE—

	shells from shrimp
1	cup water
5	black peppercorns
2	bay leaves
1	cup sweet sherry
3	tablespoons coarsely chopped onion
4	tablespoons butter
4	tablespoons flour
⅓	cup heavy cream
4	tablespoons Parmesan cheese
	salt and white pepper to taste
	dash Worcestershire sauce

1. Make stock by combining shrimp shells, water, peppercorns, bay leaves, sherry and onions. Bring to a boil, and then simmer 10 minutes. Strain through cheese cloth.
2. Preheat oven to 400°F.
3. Melt butter for sauce in a pan, add flour and stir until blended and bubbling. Stir in stock and carefully whisk in cream.
4. Add Parmesan, salt, white pepper and Worcestershire sauce, stirring until smooth. Keep warm.
5. Arrange shrimp in a shallow baking pan, drizzle with melted butter and bake for about 7 minutes.
6. To serve, place on 2 small plates and top with warm sherry sauce (do not simmer shrimp in sauce).

Serves: 2 as appetizer
Preparation: 20 minutes plus 1 hour, 10 minutes for marinating
Cooking: 30 minutes

"This is attractive to serve and it draws raves. Be sure to get the bacon crisp and do not overcook the shrimp."

PEPPERED SHRIMP

4	oz. vegetable oil
1½	cloves garlic, finely chopped
12	large shrimp, unshelled
2	oz. lemon juice
2	oz. lime juice
2	oz. dry vermouth
1	teaspoon salt
1	tablespoon coarse pepper
	lemon and lime slices for garnish

1. Heat oil to 375°F. and slightly sauté garlic until brown. Be careful.
2. Add rest of ingredients and sauté until shrimp are pink and slightly firm (about 5 to 10 minutes). Stir occasionally. Remove most of liquid.
3. Serve garnished with lemon and lime slices and some pan juices.

Serves: 1
Preparation: 5 minutes
Cooking: 5 to 10 minutes

"Delicious. Be sure to try this at home or on the boat if you can't make it to Pappas'."

SHRIMP MOUTARDE

¼ cup mayonnaise
1-2 tablespoons Dijon mustard
2 tablespoons minced onion
¾ cup finely chopped celery
18 large shrimp, peeled, deveined, and cooked
croutons for garnish

1. Preheat oven to 350°F.
2. Combine mayonnaise, mustard, onion and celery.
3. Place ⅓ of above sauce in each of 3 ramekins. Add 6 shrimp to each ramekin.
4. Top with croutons and bake for 8 to 10 minutes. Serve immediately.

Serving Suggestion: Double the sauce recipe, add 2 to 3 tablespoons milk to thin slightly, add shrimp. Place all in casserole dish, and bake for 15 to 20 minutes. Then serve over rice.

Serves: 3
Preparation: 20 minutes
Cooking: 8 to 20 minutes

"This is easy to make and QUITE tasty!"

SHRIMP ALMENDRINA

(Allow 2 hours to chill shrimp)

2	eggs
2	cups milk
2	cups flour
	salt and freshly ground pepper
2½	lbs. jumbo shrimp, peeled and deveined, tails intact
4	cups sliced almonds
	oil for deep frying
	Orange Mustard Sauce*

1. Beat the eggs until light and fluffy in medium size bowl. Stir in milk.
2. Gradually add flour, blending well. Add salt and pepper to taste.
3. Hold shrimp by tail and dip into batter, allowing excess to drip back into bowl. Do not cover tails with batter.
4. Sprinkle all sides of batter-coated shrimp with almonds. Place on cookie sheet and refrigerate at least 2 hours before frying.
5. Heat oil to 375°F. Deep fry shrimp a few at a time, just until they turn pink, about 2 minutes. Do not overcook. Drain on paper towels and keep warm until all shrimp have been cooked.
6. Serve immediately with Orange Sauce.

*See index

Serves: 6 to 8 persons
Preparation: 20 minutes (plus time for chilling)
Cooking: 2 minutes each batch

"This recipe is a must for your cooking repertoire. This is one of our favorite shrimp dishes."

SHRIMP MANALES

1	tablespoon black pepper
½	tablespoon salt
½	tablespoon white pepper
½	lb. margarine, melted
½	lb. butter, melted
2	oz. Worcestershire sauce
1½	tablespoons finely chopped garlic
½	cup lemon juice
3	lbs. shrimp, peeled and deveined

1. Preheat oven to 350°F.
2. Combine all of the ingredients except shrimp and mix well.
3. Put shrimp in casserole dish and stir in the above mixture.
4. Bake for 15 to 20 minutes or until shrimp are done.

Serves: 6
Preparation: 30 minutes
Cooking: 15 to 20 minutes

"The sauce is so delicious and abundant be sure to serve with rice or over pasta. If you serve it over pasta, this recipe could serve up to 10 people. The margarine could be replaced with all butter or vice-versa. One tablespoon black pepper is correct!"

LOBSTER
LOVER

Lobster

You just *thought* that lobster was a luxury. Early North American settlers found lobsters in such abundance that they were used for fertilizer and to feed rich people's servants. However, in time, the delicious flavor and texture of lobster caught on, and in the 1800s the commercial lobstering industry began.

Endangered Species?

Lobsters are expensive now because there seems to be fewer and fewer of them available. Pollution, man, and other predators such as cod and lobsters themselves are killing off the lobster population. There's no great family feeling among the lobster clan. The young lobsters that are hatched in the spring are often eaten by the mother or by each other. If lobsters do survive and are trapped (many live to be almost 100 years old and weigh up to 20 pounds or more), pegs are put in their claws so they can't fight with each other . . . not to protect our fingers as we had always thought.

Beware Of Poachers!

There are two main kinds of lobsters in the United States — those with claws found mainly in northern waters and spiny lobsters without claws found in southern waters. You are allowed to catch both kinds provided that you have a permit to set a trap, be it a wooden slatted one or an old gasoline barrel, and have checked with local authorities to make sure they are in season. One word of caution: don't *ever* try to take a lobster out of someone else's trap. People don't take kindly to "lobster poachers" and some have even been shot at.

Lobster Battles

There are two notorious lobster "battles" that will probably never be won. One concerns how to cook — should they be boiled or steamed, in salt or sea water? New Englanders don't think that broiling (our favorite way) even merits any discussion. The second battle concerns the size. Some people swear that any lobster over 1½ pounds is too tough to eat. Others say that's nonsense and attest to the tenderness of lobsters over 10 pounds.

How To Buy

Lobsters can be purchased in the following ways:

Fresh:
>They should be active. Test by touching their eyes. Their feelers or claws will twitch. Keep in the coldest part of the refrigerator, on a bed of seaweed if possible, and use within a short time. One pound live lobster will yield ⅓ pound cooked meat.

Cooked In Shell:
>Tail should be pressed tightly against the body and spring back sharply when pulled. Shell should be tightly attached. Keeps for 3 to 4 days in refrigerator.

Cooked Out Of Shell:
>Look for firm meat with a clean smell. Keeps for 4 days in the refrigerator.

Frozen:
>Should be no sharp odor. Keeps 1 month in freezer.

Canned:
>Should be no odor when opened. Pick over for stray shells. Keeps for 1 year on shelf. This is quite expensive and not very good.

Females are usually the most succulent. Look for feathery, fin-like appendages on their underside, or if split, look for the coral (roe) running down the side.

In general, the heavier the lobster is in relation to its size, the more tender it will be.

BLUE LAGOON
LOBSTER SALAD

2	cups cooked lobster
2	ripe pineapples
⅔	cup diced celery
½	cup macadamia nuts
¼	cup shredded coconut
⅓	cup mayonnaise
¼	cup diced kiwi fruit
	additional kiwi for garnish

1. Drain and cut lobster into bite-size pieces.
2. Cut pineapple in half lengthwise. Remove fruit from each half and save shells.
3. Cut pineapple into chunks.
4. Combine lobster, pineapple chunks, celery, macadamia nuts, coconut, mayonnaise and kiwi fruit.
5. Fill the pineapple halves with mixture and garnish with sliced kiwi. (White seedless grapes can be substituted for kiwi.)

Serves: 4
Preparation: 15 minutes
Cooking: 5 minutes

"A light, tropical salad with Hawaiian overtones."

LOBSTER THERMIDOR

2   1¼-lb. Florida lobsters, split,
    cleaned and rinsed
1   qt. water
    salt to taste
5   peppercorns
2   bay leaves
    hollandaise sauce*

1. Poach the lobster in the water, salt, bay leaves, and peppercorns for about 5 minutes or until the lobster is cooked.
2. Remove from water and reserve 2 cups of the poaching water (the stock).
3. Dice the lobster and keep warm. Rinse out the shells and reserve.

—SAUCE—

3   oz. butter
2½ oz. flour
1   cup chablis
2   cups reserved stock
½   cup Parmesan cheese
1   cup sliced mushrooms, sautéed
    in 2 tablespoons of butter
    salt and white pepper
½   teaspoon sugar
1   teaspoon Worcestershire sauce
1   teaspoon lemon juice
    dash of Accent (M.S.G.)

1. Melt the butter and stir in the flour. Cook and stir for 2 minutes.
2. Gradually add the chablis and reserved stock and cook, stirring for 1 minute. Add the mushrooms, Parmesan, salt and white pepper to taste, sugar, Worcestershire, lemon juice, and Accent.

3. Preheat oven to 400°F.
4. Line the lobster shells with the sauce. Divide the lobster meat up and put in shells. Top with more sauce.
5. Top with hollandaise sauce (about 2 to 3 tablespoons for each) and bake for 10 minutes.

*See glossary or use your favorite recipe

Serves: 2
Preparation: 30 minutes
Cooking: 20 minutes

"Non-Floridians can use any kind of lobster that is available to them. Canned mushrooms can be used (don't sauté) but fresh are better."

LOBSTER TEMPURA

2	Florida lobster tails, about 1 lb. (If you cannot get Florida lobster, substitute any lobster tails.)
¾	cup white all-purpose flour
2	eggs, beaten
1	teaspoon sake
1	cup cold water or chopped ice vegetable oil for deep frying (Sunlite preferred)

1. Remove shell from lobster. Cut lobster into bite-size pieces. Wipe excess water off each piece. Set aside.
2. Heat oil to about 360°F. Be careful as oil is very hot.

—BATTER—

3. To make batter, add eggs to flour. Mix in very cold water or ice. (Kyushu adds ice to the batter to keep cold.)
4. Add sake.
5. Mix batter as little as possible (no more than 10 to 20 seconds). Place bowl in water to keep batter very cold. Start mixing only after oil has heated up.
6. Dip lobster in flour, then in batter. Coat evenly and let excess batter drip off naturally before frying.
7. Slip pieces gently into oil with tongs, fork or chopsticks. Do not move it around until batter has cooked.
8. Continually skim the oil and pick up loose batter. Fry a few at a time until light brown.
9. Serve with Tempura Sauce*

*See index

Serves: 4
Preparation: 15 minutes
Cooking: 2 to 3 minutes

"The secret is to keep the batter very cold and the oil very hot—this will give you that wonderfully light tempura as made at Kyushu. Try other seafood and vegetables as well with this batter. Use a wok because of its large surface area and slanted sides which protect against splattering."

LOBSTER BUENA VISTA

4	8 oz. lobster tails with shells court bouillon*
3	tablespoons butter
1	lb. mushrooms, sliced
½	qt. dry white wine
½	qt. heavy cream
1	teaspoon chopped fresh thyme (or ½ teaspoon dried)
¼	lb. butter
¼	lb. flour lemon juice
2	dashes Worcestershire sauce (or to taste)

1. Cook the lobster tails in court bouillon. Drain and reserve liquid.
2. Sauté the mushrooms in the 3 tablespoons butter until they have released all their juices and the pan is almost dry.
3. Bring ½ quart of court bouillion, wine, cream, and thyme to a boil.
4. In the meantime, melt the ¼ lb. butter and stir in the flour to make a roux.* Cook for 3 minutes and gradually whisk in the liquid. Bring to a boil, stirring constantly, then remove from the heat.
5. Remove lobster meat from the shells and dice. Mix the lobster meat with the sauce.
6. Season to taste with salt and pepper, Worcestershire, and lemon juice.
7. Pile mixture into the lobster shells and quickly heat under the broiler.

*See glossary

Serves: 4
Preparation: 30 minutes
Cooking: 30 minutes

"If you use frozen lobster shells, completely defrost and pat dry before proceeding with the recipe. If you have hearty eaters plan on 2 lobster tails per person. The dish is rich so they might not eat it all, but the leftovers are heavenly!"

LOBSTER THERMIDOR "PETER'S PLACE"

1   Florida lobster, split into halves
1   cup of bechamel sauce*
2   teaspoons chopped chives
½   stick butter
2   tablespoons "good" sherry (not cooking sherry)
2   tablespoons inexpensive brandy for flaming
4   tablespoons grated Parmesan cheese
¼   cup heavy cream
4   slices Swiss or Gruyere cheese, paper thin
4   slices Canadian bacon, paper thin
     paprika
1   additional rounded tablespoon grated Parmesan cheese

1. Remove lobster meat from lobsters, after draining well.
2. Squeeze the meat to remove excess moisture. Then cut into bite-sized chunks.
3. Make the bechamel sauce and keep warm.
4. Sauté the cut-up lobster in ¼ stick melted butter. Add the chives.
5. Flame* the lobster-butter-chive mixture with the brandy.
6. Remove the lobster with a slotted spoon and place back into the lobster shells.
7. Add the butter-brandy-chive mixture to the bechamel sauce and heat.
8. Add the other ¼ stick butter to the hot bechamel sauce.
9. Add the sherry to the bechamel sauce.
10. Stir the 4 tablespoons of Parmesan into the bechamel.
11. Add the heavy cream and whisk together well.
12. Pour the bechamel mixture all over, in, and around the lobster in the shells, reserving a few tablespoons of the sauce.

13. Place 2 slices of Canadian bacon on each lobster half.
14. Place 2 slices of the cheese on top of the Canadian bacon.
15. Spread reserved bechamel on top of cheese and sprinkle with remaining Parmesan. Sprinkle paprika for color.
16. Bake for 20 minutes at 350°F. and serve.

*See glossary

Serves: 1
Preparation: 45 minutes
Cooking: 20 minutes

"Steps 1 and 2 can be done earlier in the day and the lobster meat and shells refrigerated just until ready to cook. Florida lobsters have meat only in their tails and there's not enough to refill both the body and the tail. Feel free to use just the body or just the tail to stuff and serve."

MEDAILLONS DES HOMARD AU BELUGA

—FISH FUMÉ—

1	lb. fish bones (snapper, sea bass, turbot, etc.)
½	stalk celery
½	onion
1½	large tomatoes
½	bay leaf
	salt, whole black pepper
1	pint cold water

1. Thinly slice all vegetables.
2. Put all the ingredients into a pot. Bring to boil and simmer for 30 minutes or long enough to reduce it to ⅓. Makes 1 pint.

—NANTUA SAUCE—

1	oz. soybean oil
6	New Zealand lobster tails
2	oz. white wine (California)
1½	large tomatoes, diced
1½	oz. brown roux*
1	pint Fish Fumé (see above)

1. Shell the lobster tails and set the meat aside.
2. Mix the lobster shells with all the other ingredients and cook over a medium heat for 20 minutes.
3. Skim very often and strain. Makes 1 pint.

—LOBSTER—

meat from 6 lobster tails
½	oz. shallots, chopped
2	oz. cognac
5	oz. Nantua Sauce (see above)
1½	oz. heavy cream
1	oz. soybean oil
	Beluga caviar

1. Cut the lobster meat into medallions - 4 per tail.
2. Sauté the shallots in the oil.
3. Add the lobster medallions and cook until nearly done.
4. Deglaze* with the cognac and flame*.
5. Remove the lobster and set aside.
6. Add the Nantua Sauce to the pan. Bring to a boil and add salt and pepper to taste. Turn off the heat.
7. Put the lobster back into the pan with the sauce.
8. Add the cream and top with the Beluga caviar. Serve.

*See glossary

Serves: 6
Preparation: 1 hour
Cooking: 1 hour

"You can make the Fish Fumé and Nantua Sauce ahead and refrigerate. Lobster tails other than those from New Zealand are a fine substitute. Decadently delicious!"

LOBSTER
AU COGNAC

4	6-8 oz. lobster tails
2	oz. melted butter
2	bulbs shallots, finely diced
2	tomatoes
3	oz. cognac
	salt and pepper to taste
4	oz. heavy cream
2	cups cooked rice

1. Remove lobster from shell and cut into small bite-size pieces.
2. Heat butter in a frying pan.
3. Add shallots and lobster and sauté until lobster is halfway cooked.
4. Add tomatoes to lobster.
5. Add cognac and ignite with a match. Let flame extinguish by itself.
6. Add salt and pepper.
7. Add heavy cream and cook until lobster is done.
8. On a 10-inch plate, place ½ cup of cooked rice. Pour lobster on top. Cover with sauce and serve with fresh vegetables.

Serves: 4 to 6 servings
Preparation: 10 minutes
Cooking: 10 minutes

"This recipe preserves the flavor of the lobster and is c'est magnifique!"

Notes

CRAB
DADDY

Crabs

Of some 4,500 species of crabs worldwide, two that make their home in Florida are not only easy to catch yourself but delicious to eat as well. Stone crabs are especially popular for their claws, by law the only part which may be removed, and blue crabs which are used for those tasty — and often spicy — devilled crabs so often found in Florida fish markets and seafood restaurants. There are also soft shelled crabs, the same as blue crabs except they are found and caught just after the old shell has been shed and before the new one has hardened, and spotted crabs, and . . . well, some places in Florida *do* serve Maryland steamed crabs even though they have to be imported here first.

Catch A Bucketful

It's a common sight on a summer evening to see kids or families ambling out by a pier or into a marshy area near brackish water. They'll have dip-nets and cane poles, and hunks of fish or raw chicken used as bait to catch a bucketful of blue crabs. These crustaceans aren't picky about diet—they'll eat anything and are thus a sure bet to catch if you follow a few simple rules. Approach slowly from the rear, so as not to alarm the crabs if they are feeding during an outgoing tide. If it's after sunset, carry a lantern, hold your wire basket or trap in the water, and just wait for the critters with the most curiosity to come on up. Once you feel their weight in the trap, you can scoop them up with the net and then transfer them to a tub or bucket to keep them alive until you get home and are ready to cook them.

Stone Crab Catchin'

Stone crabs require a little more preparation and knowledge. It used to be that they could be routed from their hiding holes with a J-shaped hook, but this is now illegal. Traps must be used, and a permit from the Division of Marine Resources is required regardless of whether it's for personal or commerical use. And, you're allowed to catch them only from October 15 to May 15.

Time Out!

If you're patient and like to observe nature in action, you'll probably get to witness stone crabs doing battle. Often they'll look like strange knights holding out their shields and jousting spears, as they can disengage their claws from their bodies until one gets a secure grip on the other. As in true chivalry, no harm will be done, but the loser simply drops his claw and leaves in disgrace, a vanquished foe who has lost his weapon. In time, though, the claw will regenerate, ready for another match.

Eat, Eat, Eat!

Beyond the fun of crabbing, there's the joy of eating them, whether you or your fish market have gone out for the catch. We know several Florida folks who make the rounds of their favorite seafood restaurants just so they can sample the many varieties of recipes that can be used to make Blue Crab Imperial, Devilled Crabs, Stone Crab Salad, Shrimp Stuffed with Stone Crabs, Stuffed Crab, and other popular dishes. No need ever to feel crabby about *this* seafood delight!

CRAB DIP APPETIZER

6½ oz. crab meat, white or special
½ cup sour cream
1 teaspoon lemon juice
½ teaspoon Tabasco sauce
¼ teaspoon horseradish
½ teaspoon salt
fresh chopped parsley (for garnish)
paprika (for garnish)
crackers

1. Pick through crab meat very carefully to remove all shell and cartilage.
2. Mix all ingredients together, except for parsley and paprika.
3. Place on crackers and garnish with parsley and paprika.

Serves: 6
Preparation: 15 minutes

"You can make ahead and let the flavors 'marry.' Quick and easy for unexpected company."

CRAB MEAT CANAPE LORENZO

8	oz. king crab meat
1	teaspoon butter
2	shallots, minced
¼	cup chopped green pepper
¾	cup chopped fresh mushrooms
2	tablespoons diced pimiento
¼	teaspoon English mustard
2	tablespoons sauterne
¼	cup heavy cream
2	egg yolks, lightly beaten
	dash of cayenne
	salt and pepper to taste
8	toast squares, cut in quarters
8	slices American cheese, cut in quarters

1. Preheat oven to 300°F.
2. Melt butter in skillet. Sauté shallots, green pepper and mushrooms for about 3 minutes.
3. Add pimiento, mustard and sauterne. Carefully stir in cream and remove from heat to stir into egg yolks.
4. Season to taste with salt, pepper and cayenne.
5. Spread on toast squares and top with cheese. Bake on buttered pan for 5 to 8 minutes or until cheese melts and crab is heated through.

Serves: 8 to 10 as appetizer
Preparation: 15 minutes
Cooking: 15 minutes

"This is easy! Use crab to stuff mushrooms sautéed in wine or spice it up and spread on English muffins with tomato slices topped with Swiss or Cheddar cheese."

115

CRAB SALAD A LA GRECQUE

16   oz. fresh lump crab meat
¼   cup finely chopped onion
2   tablespoons chopped parsley
1   tablespoon chopped pimiento,
      rinsed and drained
¼   cup fresh lemon juice, strained
½   cup light olive oil
½   teaspoon oregano
      salt and pepper to taste

1. Check crab meat for any shell or cartilage; place in mixing bowl.
2. Add onion, parsley and pimiento. Stir gently and set aside.
3. Make dressing by combining the fresh lemon juice, olive oil, salt and pepper and oregano; blend well with a wire whisk or in the blender.
4. Pour over crab and toss gently.
5. Refrigerate several hours.
6. To serve, place crab mixture on a plate lined with leaf lettuce; garnish with ripe olives, rose radishes, lemon wedges and parsley.

Serves: 6 as a first course, 3 as a main course
Preparation: 10 minutes (plus time for chilling)

"A light and refreshing appetizer or luncheon dish."

ARTICHOKE FELICE
WITH LOBSTER SAUCE

6	artichoke bottoms (fresh or canned)
	butter
1	cup lobster sauce*
8	oz. crab meat, picked over
2	tablespoons cognac
1	tablespoon Parmesan cheese

1. Place artichoke bottoms in generously buttered skillet and simmer until warm.
2. In a sauce pan, heat lobster sauce.
3. When very hot, add crab meat and cognac and boil 1 minute.
4. In an oven-proof pan place artichoke bottoms, stuff with crab mixture, nap with remaining sauce.
5. Sprinkle with Parmesan cheese and brown under broiler for a few minutes.

*See index for Chauveron's Lobster Sauce

Serves: 3 to 6 as first course or appetizer
Preparation and Cooking: 20 minutes

"A specialty of the house — absolutely delectable."

CAPTAIN BOB'S CRAB IMPERIAL

2   lbs. deluxe blue crab meat (or lump crab)
2   egg yolks
1½   whole eggs
¾   cups mayonnaise
1½   teaspoons Worcestershire sauce
2   dashes Tabasco sauce
      pinch thyme
1   teaspoon dry mustard
1½   teaspoons chopped parsley
1½   tablespoons grated Parmesan cheese (optional)

1. Preheat oven to 450°F.
2. Combine all ingredients and mix together.
3. Portion into individual serving dishes or place in shallow baking dish.
4. Brush lightly with mayonnaise and sprinkle with Parmesan if desired.
5. Bake 10 to 15 minutes.
6. Garnish with paprika and parsley.

Serves: 6 to 8
Preparation: 20 minutes
Cooking: 10 to 15 minutes

"If you are serving this to guests, we would recommend your buying the whole crab claws because the crab in cans is nearly impossible to pick through to get all the shells out! This dish would be attractive served in small ramekins or seashells. Can be made ahead before a dinner party, refrigerated, and popped into the oven to be served as a first (or main) course."

CRAB CAKES

2	lbs. crab meat (1 lb. special, 1 lb. claw)
2	eggs, well beaten
¾	teaspoon salt
¼	teaspoon ground red pepper
1	cup mayonnaise
½	cup grated and drained onion
4	oz. crushed saltine crackers

1. Pick over the crab meat to remove shell or cartilage.
2. Beat eggs well; add salt and ground red pepper. Beat until pepper has dissolved.
3. Add mayonnaise and drained onion to eggs and mix well. Taste for flavor.
4. Pour over crab meat, add half of cracker crumbs, and stir gently to blend, leaving the crab as whole as possible. The mixture will be rather wet and loose, but it is manageable when cakes are coated with crackers.
5. Shape into 12 oval or round crab cakes. Dredge them in the remaining cracker crumbs. Press between the hands to make the crumbs adhere and the cakes hold together.
6. Heat oil for deep frying to 325°F. and cook the cakes in a basket until golden brown all over. Drain and serve hot with tartar sauce or red chili sauce.

Serves: 4 to 6 (12 crab cakes)
Preparation: 30 minutes
Cooking: 20 minutes

"This recipe makes the lightest crab cakes we have ever tasted—and they're nearly all crab. Could be made into smaller cakes and served as an appetizer. Set some of this mixture aside and freeze. It can be used later in the recipe for Stuffed Perch Oscar (see index)."

DEVILLED CRAB MEAT

1	small onion, finely chopped
1	stalk celery, finely chopped
¼	cup finely chopped green pepper
¼	finely chopped red pepper
1	clove garlic, finely mashed
½	cup olive oil
1	lb. crab meat (fresh or frozen— picked through to remove shell)
1	tablespoon finely chopped scallions
½	teaspoon Worcestershire sauce
1	tablespoon prepared mustard dash Tabasco sauce salt and white pepper to taste
¼	cup dry sherry
¼	cup milk
2	whole eggs, lightly beaten
2	tablespoons bread crumbs paprika chopped fresh parsley (for garnish)

1. Sauté onions, celery, peppers, and garlic in olive oil until light brown in color.
2. Add crab meat, scallions, Worcestershire sauce, mustard, Tabasco, salt, pepper, sherry and milk. Bring to boil over low to medium heat.
3. Remove from heat, add eggs and bread crumbs. Mix well.
4. If using this as a main dish, place in 2-quart casserole, top with paprika and parsley, and broil for 5 to 7 minutes.
5. If using this as appetizer, serve on toast points or spoon into coquille dishes and broil for 1 to 2 minutes.
6. If using as stuffing, place in flounder and bake as usual.

Serves: 4 (as a main dish)
Preparation: 20 minutes
Cooking: 10 to 15 minutes

"Excellent and very versatile dish."

CRAB QUICHE

—ONE-CRUST PIE SHELL—
1 cup sifted all-purpose flour
½ scant teaspoon salt
⅓ cup shortening (half butter and half Crisco at room temperature and blended together)
2-3 tablespoons ice water

1. Preheat oven to 425°F.
2. Chill flour in refrigerator for about 5 minutes.
3. Sift flour and salt together.
4. Cut shortening into sifted flour with a pastry blender or your fingertips until the mixture is partially blended.
5. Sprinkle the ice water over the flour mixture, blending lightly with your fingers and adding only enough water to obtain a dough that holds together.
6. Roll the dough into a ball and refrigerate wrapped in wax paper for at least 2 hours.
7. Roll dough out to approximately ⅛ inch thick.
8. Place in a greased pie plate or quiche pan, making a rim with your fingers or trimming the edge of the dough to fit the pan.
9. Prick dough all over with a fork and cover with a 14-inch circle of wax paper. Fill with raw rice or uncooked beans.
10. Bake about 15 minutes.
11. Remove rice or beans and wax paper. Cool.

—CRAB QUICHE FILLING—

3	eggs
¾	cup light cream
1	cup lump crab meat, picked over partially baked pie shell
¼	cup grated Swiss cheese
1	pinch each salt and pepper
2	drops Tabasco sauce
2	tablespoons chives or scallions, chopped

1. Preheat oven to 350°F.
2. Beat eggs. Add cream and blend well.
3. Place crab meat in bottom of pie shell and sprinkle with cheese.
4. Mix together salt, pepper, Tabasco, chives or scallions and add to crab meat.
5. Pour cream and egg mixture over all.
6. Bake 35 to 40 minutes or until knife inserted in middle comes out dry.
7. Cool 10 minutes before serving.

Serves: 4
Preparation: Shell - 10 minutes, quiche - 10 minuntes
Cooking: Shell - 15 minutes, quiche - 35 to 40 minutes

"A light luncheon or Sunday supper dish. Serve with a green salad or tomatoes and basil with vinaigrette."

CRAB POT
FAMOUS CRAB CAKES

4	lbs. crab meat, shredded
1	lb. crab meat, lump
5	eggs
30	crushed crackers
1	cup mayonnaise
5	tablespoons Worcestershire sauce
	fresh parsley, chopped
1	cup prepared mustard
	salt
5	tablespoons Old Bay seasoning
	vegetable oil for frying

1. Preheat oven to 200°F.
2. Pick over crab meat very carefully to remove shells and cartilage.
3. Beat eggs.
4. Using a flat pan, add the 4 pounds shredded crab meat.
5. Spread evenly in the pan.
6. Add the crackers, mayonnaise, eggs, Worcestershire sauce, parsley, mustard, salt, and the seasonings. Mix well with your hands.
7. Add the lump crab meat. Shuffle into the mixture gently.
8. Form into 30 cakes and dust with flour.
9. Fry at about 350°F. for about 3 minutes on each side until golden brown.
10. Keep warm in the oven.

Serves: 8 to 10 as main course
Preparation: 20 minutes
Cooking: 20 minutes

"Spicy and delicious—said to be the best in the Sunshine State! you can reduce the proportions to suit your fancy, but this recipe is well-suited to a party crowd. You can always freeze part and save it for future party hors d'ouevres."

123

CRAB NORFOLK

1½-2 tablespoons butter, melted
7-8 oz. lump crab meat, remove
     cartilage
     salt and pepper to taste
     Accent to taste
1   oz. white wine

1. Place melted butter in a skillet in which the crab is to be served.
2. Add crab meat. Season with salt, pepper, and Accent.
3. Sauté over medium-high heat until bubbly and lightly browned. Fluff up carefully without disturbing crab lumps.
4. Turn over and cook again until lightly brown.
5. As you remove skillet from the stove, quickly pour wine around the edges (may use less than 1 ounce). As it bubbles and sizzles, serve. This is a dish that will not wait.

Serves: 1
Preparation: 10 minutes
Cooking: 10 to 15 minutes

"Michael Wolchik, owner of the Sea Grill, says Crab Norfolk is a recipe originated by his grandfather. You'll enjoy this classic favorite of Floridians!"

ALASKAN KING CRAB LEGS DIJONAISE

9-12 3" pieces king crab legs removed from shell
1 4-oz. jar Dijon mustard (Grey Poupon)
1 cup seasoned bread crumbs
¼ teaspoon garlic powder
¼ lb. butter
1 cup bearnaise sauce*
½ cup fresh whipped cream
   chopped parsley
   parsley sprig

1. Dredge crab legs in mustard. Lightly roll in bread crumbs, sprinkled with garlic powder.
2. Sauté in butter until browned. Place in individual baking dishes.
3. Mix bearnaise with whipped cream. Nap the crab legs.
4. Place under broiler until golden brown. Garnish with chopped parsley and one sprig of parsley.

*See glossary

Serves: 3 to 4
Preparation: 10 minutes
Cooking: 10 minutes

"This is an easy but elegant dish. Garnish appropriately."

CRAB CANNELONI

8 canneloni shells
1 lb. fresh spinach, blanched and chopped
1 oz. butter
½ cup finely shredded onion
1 clove garlic, finely chopped
2 oz. Pernod
¼ pint heavy cream
4 egg yolks
4 oz. crab meat, picked through thoroughly
  salt and pepper to taste
  nutmeg
  homemade tomato sauce (your favorite recipe)

1. Prepare canneloni according to package directions. Drain.
2. Squeeze spinach to remove moisture. Set aside.
3. Brown butter in large skillet.
4. Add onion and garlic. Cook until transparent.
5. Add Pernod and flame* dry.
6. Add cream and spinach to mixture.
7. Bring to simmer.
8. Add egg yolks and stir. Add crab meat.
9. Add salt, pepper and nutmeg.
10. Stuff skins according to package directions. Serve with fresh tomato sauce on top. Be sure it's hot!

*See glossary

Preparation: 15 minutes
Cooking: 20 minutes

"The Pier House makes their own canneloni shells. You can make your own or purchase them ready made. Or try this popular dish at the Pier House or 'to go' from their new gourmet deli."

SOFT SHELL
CRABS CHERVIL

18-24	soft shell crabs
	salt and pepper to taste
	Worcestershire sauce
	flour for dredging
4	eggs
	clarified butter* for frying
2-3	shallots, finely chopped
2-3	oz. white wine
½	cup chervil (fresh if possible, or 2
	teaspoons dried)
	hollandaise sauce*

1. Wash soft shell crabs gently and very thoroughly. Pat dry.
2. Marinate in small amount of salt, pepper and Worcester-shire.
3. Dip each crab into flour (lightly), then into egg batter.
4. Dip into flour again.
5. Pour clarified butter ¼" deep into skillet and heat to about 400°F. This is very hot, so be careful.
6. Place crabs in skillet and cook quickly. Turn once and reduce temperature. Finish cooking slowly. (Either place lid on skillet and cook slowly or place in oven and cook slowly for about 5 minutes.)
7. Remove crabs and place on serving tray.
8. Remove all but 1 to 2 tablespoons of butter from skillet.
9. To remaining butter add shallots. Fry to a golden brown.
10. Add wine and chervil to skillet, reduce heat, and warm through.

11. Mix with hollandaise sauce in a separate bowl.
12. Spread ½ the sauce mixture over crab and pass the remaining sauce separately.

*See glossary

Serves: 4 to 6
Preparation: 15 minutes
Cooking: 15 to 20 minutes

"Try these chervil-kissed crabs at home or at the Seaport Inn, considered to be one of Florida's top seafood restaurants."

CRAB TRAP
CRAB CRÊPES

—CRÊPE BATTER—
¾ cup sifted flour
½ teaspoon salt
2 eggs, beaten
1 cup milk
1 teaspoon melted butter

1. Combine flour, salt, eggs and milk. Blend until smooth.
2. Add melted butter and blend. Let stand several hours.
3. Heat a 5" skillet. Using about 2 tablespoons crêpe batter for crêpe, spread evenly by tilting pan. Brown crêpe on both sides.
4. As each crêpe is done, place in separate pan. Cover to keep warm.

—CRÊPE FILLING—
2 tablespoons butter
2 tablespoons flour
½ teaspoon Tabasco sauce
¼ teaspoon Worcestershire sauce
½ teaspoon dry mustard
½ teaspoon salt
1 cup evaporated milk
2 tablespoons Parmesan cheese
1 tablespoon cream sherry wine
12 oz. blue crab meat (preferably fresh)—pick through thoroughly light cream

—FILLING—

1. Melt butter. Add flour, Tabasco, Worcestershire, mustard and salt. Blend slowly. Add evaporated milk. Stir until thick.
2. Remove from heat. Stir in Parmesan and cream sherry to make crêpe sauce.
3. Add ¼ cup of crêpe sauce to the crab meat and mix.
4. Place 3 tablespoons or 1½ oz. of crab meat mixture into crêpe. Gently roll up.
5. Place rolled crêpe in shallow baking dish. Thin remaining sauce with some light cream and gently spoon over crêpes. Bake at 400°F. for 10 to 12 minutes.

Serves: 4 to 6
Preparation: 15 minutes (plus 2 to 3 hours for crêpes to set)
Cooking: 15 minutes crêpes/20 minutes filling

"Your guests will compliment you. While you're at The Crab Trap, be sure to try the sautéed turtle!"

SOFT SHELL CRABS WITH LEMON GINGER SAUCE

12	small soft shell crabs
1½	cups plus 1 tablespoon cornstarch
4	tablespoons soy sauce
4	tablespoons sake
3	eggs
1	tablespoon sesame oil
1	cup rice powder (available in Oriental food markets)
	peanut oil for deep frying
2	teaspoons chopped green chili pepper
½	cup coarsely chopped Chinese bok choy
½	cup thinly sliced white onions
½	cup red peppers in ¼" slices
½	cup snow peas
4	oz. water chestnuts, chopped
4	oz. bean sprouts
1	teaspoon minced fresh garlic
1	lemon (peeled, reserve rind)
1	teaspoon minced fresh ginger (available in Oriental food markets)
1½	cups chicken stock
1	teaspoon brown sugar
	water

1. Clean crabs thoroughly.
2. Mix until smooth: ½ cup corn starch with 3 tablespoons soy sauce and 3 tablespoons sake. Add eggs and sesame oil.
3. Dip crabs into batter.
4. Next, dust crabs in mixture of 1 cup cornstarch and rice powder.
5. Deep fry at 375° F. in peanut oil in deep skillet until golden brown.
6. Heat peanut oil in wok. As oil gets hot add chili pepper, bok choy, onions, red peppers and snow peas.
7. Stir fry until tender but crisp.
8. Add water chestnuts and bean sprouts. Stir together, then push to side of wok.
9. Prepare mixture of chicken stock, 1 tablespoon of soy sauce and 1 tablespoon sake.
10. Place garlic, lemon rind and ginger in oil.
11. Add chicken stock mixture to wok.
12. Add juice from lemon and brown sugar. Mix.
13. Spoon out portion (about ½ cup) of this sauce for dip (on side).
14. To thicken sauce in pan, prepare mixture of 1 tablespoon cornstarch and 1 tablespoon water. Add to sauce in wok. (If too thick, add chicken stock.)
15. Push vegetables back into sauce. Mix with sauce.
16. Place vegetables on serving plates. Arrange crabs on plates. Pour sauce on crabs. Serve dip sauce on side.

Serves: 4
Preparation: 10 minutes
Cooking: 10 minutes

"Enjoy by the poolside at the Terraza or at home in your back yard."

NOBODY SHUCKS
LIKE ME

Oysters

Shellfish With A Pedigree

Throughout history, this bisexual, vegetarian bivalve has been providing man with high nutrition, food for thought, and maybe even aphrodisical prowess. Cavemen relished them. The Chinese, 2,000 years ago, devoured them.Cicero ate oysters to nourish his eloquence. The Greeks and Romans wouldn't think of throwing a banquet without providing their guests with dozens of oysters on the half shell as a "starter." Louis XI of France insisted that his close group of "great men" of the Sorbonne swallow a certain amount of them per day to make them bright and keep them so.

Big Drinkers!

Baby oysters, called spat, are conceived in the water, far from their mothers and fathers and are free swimmers. They then grow a strong foot and after two weeks attach themselves to the first clean hard object they bump into. From that time on, the oysters devote themselves to hanging on and drinking — up to 26 to 27 quarts of water an hour. From the stream of water passing through their gills they strain the diatoms and perida which are nourished by various minerals in the water. This is reflected in the oysters' food value, flavor, and color. If the oysters were transplanted from polluted water to a clean spot, they could cleanse their bodies of pollutants within two weeks.

Oysters are considered one of the most nutritious foods available; they're full of minerals, vitamins, proteins, and glycogens. And they're not fattening!

A He . . . Or A She??

Alas, the poor oyster never knows whether it is a he or a she, as from time to time, he (or she) changes his sex and performs whatever function is required at the time. As a he, it sends out a little potent gush of milt to excite a female into spawning 5 to 50 million eggs. If the tide is right the milt meets the eggs, and spat result.

In cooler waters to the north, oysters take from two to three years to mature, but in the southern waters they reach market size in a year—sometimes even in nine months.

None Better!

In Florida and the south we have what are known as Eastern oysters. The Apalachicola natural oyster beds have for years provided excellent oysters in great numbers and are the most well known of Florida's oyster crop. Other areas of Florida produce them as well: some coming from the east coast around Grant, near Melbourne, which boasts oysters that are particularly large for southern waters. Ask any oyster eater from Florida what he thinks of his local oysters, and he will say, "They're the best; they're none better!" Also available in Florida marketplaces are imports from Louisiana and Texas.

Versatile, Too!

Oysters are such a versatile food. They can be served raw on the half shell or as a cocktail, stewed, steamed, fried, baked or broiled, barbequed, pickled, spiced, or smoked. They can be purchased live in the shell, fresh or frozen shucked, canned, or frozen and breaded.

Tap Them To Test Them

When purchasing oysters alive in their shells, look for ones tightly closed. If they are open, tap them and they should quickly close. If they don't, pass them up. You can keep them for seven to ten days in the refrigerator. Large oysters are known as "select"; average ones, "standards."

Freshly shucked oysters should be plump and have a natural creamy color and clear liquid. Plump oyster meat is a sign of good quality. They are available in pints, quarts, and gallons. Freshly shucked oysters maintain their quality for about a week if they are packed in ice in the refrigerator. Frozen oysters can be purchased and kept for up to two months in the freezer. It is not recommended that you freeze them at home; packers have "quick freeze" facilities which are not possible with home freezers.

Watch It

The State of Florida has stringent regulations on oyster harvesting and marketing—all for the benefit of the consumer. Waters where harvesting is done are inspected regularly to make sure they are free from pollutants. Rules require harvesters and packers to have sanitary conditions and to chill the oysters

135

immediately. Canned oysters must have a date printed on the can to show a two-week shelf life.

Eat Your Heart Out

In Florida, a fairly regular supply of oysters is available throughout the year, with the possible exception of the summer months. Fall and winter are traditional oyster-eating times. The "R" month tradition avoids harvesting and storage problems during the warm months and protects the oysters during summer spawning.

How Many Does It Take?

How many oysters should you buy for your family or dinner party? If served as an appetizer, a half dozen per person should be ample. If raw oysters are served as the main dish, allow one to three dozen per person. If prepared with vegetables and other foods, a quart of shucked oysters should serve six people.

Plucking And Shucking

But, you say, you want to harvest your own oysters? Fine, but first check with the Florida Marine Patrol or your local health department. They have maps telling you where you can find the tasty delicacies and whether the area is open or closed. Once that's done, arm yourself with a pail, work gloves, and sneakers. Go down at low tide, and you can see them clinging to the mudbanks or in the marshes. Sometimes they are just above the water; sometimes just under. Be sure to wear your gloves because often the edges of the oysters are very sharp.

Nobody Shucks Like You!

Now you've got them home. How do you open them? No problem, but it does take just a little practice. Again, wearing gloves, place the oyster mound side down. With a hammer or oyster opener, chip off the excess lip until you can see the separation between the shells. Force the tip of your oyster knife into the separation and slide it up under until you can slice the muscle. Do the same on the upper side. Take off the upper shell, and there you have the oyster ready for anything— especially eating!

As Jonathan Swift once said, "He was a bold man that first eat a oyster." And thank goodness, someone did!

136

OYSTER POT PIE

4	slices bacon, finely chopped
4	tablespoons butter
⅔	cup minced onion
8	drops Tabasco sauce
4	tablespoons lemon juice
1½	lbs. oysters (reserve liquor)
2	teaspoons salt
1	teaspoon garlic powder
1	teaspoon seafood seasoning (such as Old Bay)
12	oz. mushrooms, sliced
¼	cup Rhine wine
½	cup cooked white or brown rice baked pie crust top

1. Cook bacon until just crisp. Remove from pan. Pour off most of the fat. Don't wipe the pan out as the small amount of bacon fat helps the flavor.
2. Melt butter in same pan.
3. Sauté onions until just transparent. Add Tabasco and lemon juice.
4. Season oysters with salt, garlic powder, and seafood seasoning.
5. Let oysters come to room temperature before proceeding.
6. Add the mushrooms and wine and simmer for a few minutes until mushrooms begin to soften.
7. Add bacon and oysters. Cook for 2 to 3 minutes. Don't overcook the oysters.
8. Add cooked rice. Stir carefully and remove from the heat.
9. Cover and keep off the heat for 10 to 15 minutes.
10. If mixture seems to need more moisture, add some of the reserved oyster liquor.
11. Place in 8 to 10-ounce earthenware casserole dish. Put pastry crust on top.
12. Place in hot oven (450 to 500°F.) just long enough to heat through.

Serves: 4 to 5
Preparation: 15 minutes
Cooking: 20 minutes

"Good as a luncheon dish or Sunday supper. Serve with salad or cole slaw and a rich dessert."

OYSTERS OREGANATI

30   oysters, well drained—either
      canned or fresh shucked
½   tablespoon chopped garlic
4   tablespoons bread crumbs
1   tablespoon oregano
1   tablespoon Romano cheese,
      freshly grated
4   whole canned tomatoes,
      chopped
      olive oil

1. Shuck oysters and drain well. Put shucked oysters in shallow baking dish.
2. Add garlic. Sprinkle with oregano, chopped tomato, bread crumbs and Romano cheese. Sprinkle with small amount of olive oil.
3. Bake until golden brown at 400°F. for about 10 minutes.

Serves: 5 as an appetizer or 2 to 3 as a main dish
Preparation: 15 minutes without having to shuck oysters
            45 minutes with shucking oysters
Cooking: 10 minutes

"You might try this with the oysters in their half shells. It would look elegant, and as a finger hors d'oeuvre it would be easier to eat. The aroma that this dish sends off transports you right to Italy!"

OYSTERS ROCKEFELLER

	rock salt
18	oysters in shells, opened—save liquor
	oyster liquor
½	lb. fresh spinach (or frozen chopped)
4	tablespoons butter or margarine, softened
½	cup finely chopped scallions
1	teaspoon celery salt
¾	teaspoon garlic salt
½	teaspoon white pepper
½	teaspoon salt
2-3	squirts Tabasco sauce
1-2	tablespoons Anisette
	bread crumbs, very fine
	Parmesan cheese

1. Put enough rock salt in a large baking pan so that half-shelled oysters can rest without tipping.
2. Open oysters, leaving them on the half shell and reserving the oyster liquor. Place oysters on rock salt in baking pan.
3. Wash and chop fresh spinach. Cook in oyster liquor just until wilted. (If spinach is frozen, cook in oyster liquor until just defrosted.) Drain well and squeeze to remove excess moisture. Process slightly or chop well.
4. Add soft butter or margarine and scallions to cooked spinach.
5. Add celery salt, garlic salt, pepper, salt, Tabasco sauce, Anisette, and mix well.
6. Add enough very fine bread crumbs to mixture so that stuffing can be molded into small patties, one for each oyster.
7. Place a patty on each oyster and smooth over top.
8. Broil 3 to 4 minutes. Remove from oven. Cover with cheese. Broil again until cheese melts to a light brown. Serve immediately.

Serves: 3 to 4
Preparation: 1 hour (including shucking oysters)
Cooking: approximately 8 minutes.

"Serve on rock salt on individual plates, garnished with parsley. Very elegant. Can use this same filling for clams (Clams Rockefeller). One of the best versions of Oysters Rockefeller anywhere!"

HUITRES
AU CHAMPAGNE
(Fresh Oysters with Champagne)

12	fresh oysters
1	shallot, minced
1	cup heavy cream
½	cup champagne
1	tablespoon sweet butter

1. Shuck the oysters, being careful to preserve the juice. Wash the shells and save. The cooked oysters will be served in the original shells.
2. Place the oysters in a sauce pan with the oyster juice and cook for 2 to 3 minutes.
3. Remove the oysters and keep warm.
4. Add the cream, champagne and the minced shallot to the hot oyster juice. Cook over a medium heat until the sauce is reduced by one-third.
5. Swirl in the butter.
6. Taste and correct the seasoning if necessary.
7. Serve the oysters in the shells with a bit of the sauce in each one.

Serves: 2 as an appetizer
Preparation: 15 minutes
Cooking: 10 minutes

"You can garnish this dish with caviar to make it extra sumptuous. This dish is particularly delicious when served with the same champagne used in its preparation."

OYSTERS PROVENÇALE

6   oysters
     Tomato Concasse (see below)
     Parmesan cheese, grated
     Swiss cheese, grated
     mozzarella, grated

1. Open the oysters and discard the top shells. Rest the oysters on rock salt spread on flat pan or oven-proof baking dish. Top each oyster with the Tomato Concasse and the cheeses.
2. Put under the broiler until the cheese is browned—no more than 8 minutes.

—TOMATO CONCASSE—
fresh tomatoes, peeled, seeded
and diced
scallions or shallots, chopped
pepper and Italian seasoning to
taste

1. Combine all of the ingredients and bring to a boil.
2. Cool slightly.

Serves: 1 (or more depending upon the amount of oysters used)
Preparation: 10 minutes
Cooking: 15 minutes (oysters and Concasse)

"It is easier to grate the Swiss and mozzarella if they are put in the freezer for awhile. There are no precise amounts of ingredients given as this is a creative 'to taste' recipe."

OYSTERS CALYPSO

12   fresh shucked oysters with their half shell
¼   cup sugar
¼   cup hot water
2   oz. fresh ginger root, minced fine
1   bunch fresh coriander, chopped (cilantro or parsley may be substituted)
½   cup white vinegar
½   cup fresh pineapple, diced ⅛"

1. Place fresh oysters on the half shell on crushed ice and refrigerate.
2. Dissolve sugar in hot water. Add ginger root, coriander, and vinegar and mix until well blended.
3. To serve, top each oyster with 1 teaspoon of diced pineapple. Dress liberally with well-blended ginger root and coriander mixture. Serve well chilled.

Serves: 2
Preparation: 15 minutes (plus chilling time)

"Diehards may go back to their cocktail sauce, but this is a celebration! Be sure to loosen the oyster from its shell before dressing."

SCALLOPED OYSTERS

5	oz. ripe olives, cut in large pieces
1	qt. oysters
1	cup butter
½	cup finely chopped onion
1	teaspoon finely chopped garlic
1½	cups flour
½	tablespoon paprika
¼	tablespoon salt
½	teaspoon pepper
1	tablespoon Worcestershire sauce
	scant ¼ cup lemon juice
2-3	cups chicken broth
1	cup cracker crumbs

1. Preheat oven to 350°F.
2. Heat oysters in own liquid for 5 minutes. Drain, reserve liquid, and coarsely cut oysters.
3. Melt butter and cook onion and garlic over low heat until tender-crisp.
4. Gradually add flour, stirring constantly until the mixture is golden.
5. Remove from heat and stir in paprika, salt and pepper.
6. Combine reserved oyster liquid and chicken broth to make 1¼ quarts. Add to flour mixture along with Worcestershire and lemon juice.
7. Stir until smooth. Gently stir in oysters and olives and heat through.
8. Pour into casserole dish and top with crumbs.
9. Bake until it just bubbles.

Serves: 6
Preparation: 15 minutes
Cooking: 20 minutes (depending upon how long it takes to bubble)

"This is a delicious version of scalloped oysters that uses unorthodox ingredients and cooking methods. We think that you will enjoy it. Serve with crisp bread and a hearty dessert."

KEY WEST BENEDICT

	hollandaise sauce*
4	fresh broccoli spears
¼	cup clarified* butter
1	clove garlic, minced
16	oysters
4	English muffins
8	slices Canadian bacon
8	eggs
	tomato wedges
	parsley
2	green olives, sliced

1. Prepare hollandaise sauce (with extra lemon to taste).
2. Poach broccoli spears.
3. Place butter and garlic in sauté pan.
4. Add oysters and sauté until warm.
5. Split muffins and grill. Top with Canadian bacon. Set aside.
6. Poach eggs.
7. Place muffins topped with bacon on serving plate. Place 2 oysters on each piece of bacon.
8. Gently place 1 egg on each muffin and cover with hollandaise sauce.
9. Garnish with broccoli spears and tomato wedges.
10. Sprinkle each serving with parsley and ½ slice of olive.

*See glossary

Serves: 4
Preparation: 30 minutes
Cooking: 20 minutes

"This is a favorite of the Key West locals."

145

OYSTERS MOSCOW

6   oysters
white horseradish
sour cream
buttermilk
caviar

1. Open the oysters and discard the top shells.
2. Combine 1 part horseradish, 1 part sour cream and 1 part buttermilk (about 4 to 5 tablespoons of each). Refrigerate this sauce for a little while to give the flavors a chance to blend.
3. Top each oyster with a little caviar and sauce.

Serves: 1
Preparation: 1 minute (plus time for "marriage" of flavors)

"This is so rich that you really should not have more than 6 oysters per person. If you run out of sauce, it takes no time at all to make some more (you'll have to forego the "marriage"). If you have any leftover sauce, it is very good over chopped lettuce."

**STEAMED
CLAM**

Clams

Not Just Wampum!

Americans eat lots of clams. Europeans often disdain them, feeling that perhaps the eating habits of the early colonists in America were unduly influenced by the American Indians. The Indians were avid clam eaters and showed the new arrivals how to gather, cook, and eat the tasty delights. Lucky for us! In fact, the Indians were so impressed with clams that they used the purple interior of the quahog shell as their most valuable wampum currency.

There are hundreds of different kinds of clams in North American waters, but we eat only a few types, mainly because they're the ones most easily gathered and marketed. There are the hard-shelled quahogs, the steamers, surf clams, the west coast pismo and razor, to mention a few.

Quahog clams have different names depending upon the size:

Littlenecks—1½ inches across

Cherrystones—2 inches across

Mediums and Chowders—3 inches and more across

Cherrystones and littlenecks can be eaten raw. The mediums can be steamed and served on the half shell with melted butter or used in Rhode Island or Manhattan clam chowder. The large chowder clams can be chopped up and used in New England clam chowder or stuffed.

Florida has some very large quahogs. There is no permit or size regulation for you to gather them yourself. But check with the local health department or the Florida Marine Patrol to make sure that the area is open and free from pollution.

Underground Residents

Clams live in harbors, bays, creeks, and inlets. To find quahogs, go out at low tide with a sack and a clam rake. Keep your eye on the seagulls because they know the best places to find them. On a dry beach look for small holes or squirts of water in the sand. You may have to go out into shallow water and feel around with your toes. Dig with your fingers or the rake to pry them out. If you find one, there will usually be others nearby.

There is no commercial harvesting of clams in Florida to speak of. Those sold fresh in the markets are from New England—usually steamers and cherrystones.

Clams—In The Shell Or Off The Shelf

Clams can be purchased live in the shell, already shucked, or canned. Clam broth, juice and nectar are sold bottled or canned. Buy live clams only if the shells are tightly closed. If a tap on their shells makes them close, they're all right too. Clams are sold by the dozen, the pound or in pecks and bushels. They can be kept alive several days if they are refrigerated at 32°F.

Shucked clams should be plump, sweet smelling, and free of air holes. The liquid should be clear or opalescent and have no shell particles. Shucked clams are available in waxed or metal containers that usually have see-through covers so you can check them out. At home they will keep for five days if refrigerated.

For six people, buy at least three dozen in the shell or one quart shucked or two 7-ounce cans.

Make 'Em Come Clean

Fresh clams can be very sandy, to say the least. To clean them, wash in several waters. Soak them in a cold brine (⅓ cup salt to each gallon of water). Sprinkle ¼ cup cornmeal on the top for each quart of clams. Let them remain in this brine solution for three to 12 hours. This whitens them, rids them of sand and the black material in their stomachs. After this soaking, wash them again in clear water. Discard any that float or that have broken shells.

Easy Does It!

If you are going to use the clams in chowders, steam or simmer them in a covered pot* just until the shells open. Discard any clams that don't open. Save the liquid and strain for sauces.

To make them easier to open, put the clams in the freezer for a few minutes, just until they lose the will to "clam shut." Open the clams over a container so that you can catch the liquid. Slip

---

*Clams (and mussels) can also be "steamed" in a 350°F. oven. Place in a single layer in a large pan, add some wine or water and cover tightly with aluminum foil. They should start opening after 5 to 10 minutes.

149

a thin knife in at the siphon (rounded) edge of the clam. Keep tight against the bottom. Slide the knife towards the muscle that fastens to the shell and sever. Slide the knife around and pry open. This procedure takes some practice to do quickly.

Small And Quick—Means Tender

Clams can be served on the half shell, in chowders, steamed, curried, stewed, scalloped, fried, broiled, baked, creamed, stuffed, in casseroles, on spaghetti, as fritters, in pies—and a clambake wouldn't be one without them! These naturally plump tasty creatures are eaten raw more than any other way, so when you cook them, do it for only a very short time, otherwise they become tough and rubbery. Keep in mind, the larger the clam, the tougher the meat. So save the big ones for your chowders. Clams may be substituted for oysters in recipes, but clams cook much quicker.

CLAMS CASINO

4	lbs. fresh, hand-shucked clams (about 60-80 half-shell clams, depending on size), chopped or ground up, reserve shells
1	lb. butter or margarine
¼	cup Worcestershire sauce
¼	cup chopped parsley
4	cups finely chopped green peppers
2	cups finely chopped red onions
1	teaspoon mace
⅛	cup Old Bay seafood seasoning
6	eggs
¼	cup lemon juice
1	tube anchovy paste
1-2	cups bread crumbs
	bacon strips on top

1. Grind or mince clams in blender.
2. Mix all other ingredients in a separate bowl.
3. With a tablespoon, scoop one spoon clams per half clam shell.
4. Place a spoon of batter dressing and a small strip of bacon on top of the clam.
5. Broil on middle rack until browned, heated through to bottom of clams.

Serves: 8 to 10
Preparation: Shucking takes a long time, plus 20 minutes
Cooking: 5 minutes

"This is delicious. It might be worthwhile to pay extra to have the fish store open them for you."

151

GARLIC CLAM DIP

1	6½-oz. can chopped clams
2	tablespoons clam broth (reserved from clams)
1	8-oz. package cream cheese, softened
½	tablespoon finely chopped shallots
1	tablespoon Worcestershire sauce
1	teaspoon chopped chives (dried or fresh)
1	teaspoon Beau Monde seasoning
1	clove fresh garlic, minced
	chives for garnish

1. Drain clams, reserving clam juice.
2. Combine cream cheese and clam juice in separate bowl.
3. Mix the remaining ingredients together. Beat into cream cheese mixture. Add clams.
4. Chill and garnish with chives.
5. Serve with crackers or fresh vegetable dippers.

Serves: 6 to 8
Preparation: 10 minutes (plus time for chilling)

"Great flavorful dip with lots of juicy clams!"

STEAMED CLAMS
(MINORCAN STYLE)

1	dozen clams (in shell)
2	oz. butter
4	onions, sliced ¼" thick
2	oz. Worcestershire sauce
2	stalks celery, cut in half
	fresh whole black pepper

1. Combine all ingredients in a large kettle with shallow layer of salted water. Be sure that the clams have been cleaned well.
2. Cover and steam for 8 to 10 minutes or until all the clams are opened. Discard any that haven't opened.
3. Place steamed clams in a shallow dish and pour broth over them.

Serves: 1
Preparation: 5 minutes
Cooking: 8 to 10 minutes

"The Ponce family, who claim to be direct descendents of Ponce de Leon, sent the message, 'You'll enjoy this old Minorcan speciality; our customers do!' They're right. It's great!"

CLAMS
WITH WHITE SAUCE
(NEOPOLITAN FISHERMAN STYLE)

18	fresh littleneck clams, shucked and coarsely chopped
	Italian parsley, chopped—to taste
4	garlic cloves, chopped
1	pinch white pepper
1	anchovy fillet (canned in olive oil), chopped
¼	cup olive oil
1	pinch granulated garlic powder
1	cup very light broth (chicken broth or diluted clam juice), warmed
½	lb. linguine, cooked al dente*

1. Add oil to skillet and bring almost to a sizzling point.
2. Add the chopped garlic, anchovy and parsley and cook until brown.
3. Add the chopped clams. Simmer for about 5 minutes.
4. Add the white pepper, the granulated garlic powder and the warmed broth. Let cook for a few moments, just until flavors are mixed. Taste for seasoning.
5. Serve over linguine.

*See glossary

Serves: 2
Preparation: 15 minutes
Cooking: 8 to 10 minutes

"Chef Salvatore Ponzo suggests you add 2 leaves of fresh basil to the sauce for a little different taste. It is the addition of the anchovy that makes this version of clam sauce Neopolitan. The chef also suggests you save 6 of the clams, steam them open separately, and add them, in their shells, to the dish at the very last minute."

CLAMS
WITH RED SAUCE

Follow the recipe for Clams with White Sauce Neopolitan Fisherman Style except: instead of broth add 2 cups of your favorite marinara sauce.

Notes

Notes

WALLOP
SCALLOP

Scallops

Space Age Shellfish?

Scallops are the liveliest of all the bivalves. Unlike their cousin, the oyster, they are very active swimmers. They lend new meaning to the term "jet propelled," as they snap their shells together, expelling a jet of water that acts as their means of propulsion. Sometimes on a clear day you can see them in tide pools skipping about, almost gaily, and snapping their shells in great glee. If captured, they beat their valves wildly in an attempt to escape, sounding like clacking false teeth.

It is their adductor muscle that enables them to open and close their shells so rapidly, and it is this enlarged muscle that provides us with the lean, light, firm meat with such a delicate sweet flavor.

Gourmet's Treat

Not only is the scallop a gourmet's treat, its shell is a work of art. They come in a myriad of colors—from white to black, in browns, tans, reds, purples and steely blues. The lovely shells, known as Coquilles St. Jacques, were emblematic of pilgrims who visited the shrine of St. James of Compostella. The pilgrims were required to eat the mollusks as penance, and afterward they fastened the shells to their hats. Later, those who wore the shells were recognized as crusaders who had visited the Holy Land. Later still, the shells appeared in heraldry and are seen in the crests of many famous families. And we all know the oil company that has adopted the shape as its symbol and dotted the roadsides with its signs in the shape of a scallop shell.

Scallops are responsible for the cooking term, "scalloped," which originally meant seafood that was creamed, heated, and served in the shell. Another term, "scalloped edge," refers to a pleasingly waved margin on paper.

Scallops have high levels of well-balanced protein, very little fat, and many essential minerals and vitamins. And they contain only 23 calories per ounce.

Scallops can be cooked in so many ways: scalloped, deep fried, broiled, sautéed, as kebobs, used in cocktails, stuffings, soups, and salads. In fact, they can be used in any recipe for fish salads or creamed fish.

They'll Escape!

You may catch scallops yourself in most places along the coast of Florida all year round, but check with your local Florida Marine Patrol first to make sure that the season is open. The best way to go after them is with mask and fins. Attach a sack to your waist and paddle through the eel grass in shallow water, plucking them from the grass or grabbing them as they swim by. Keep them in the water as long as possible. They may be eaten raw directly from the water. But be sure to cook them very soon, as they die when they are removed from water.

It's A Snap!

At home, scrub them thoroughly. You can put them in a 300°F. oven, deep shell down, until they open. Or insert a knife between the shells near the base of the scallop. Toss away the top shell and the dark mass that surrounds the white muscle. Carve the muscle out.

How Sweet They Are!

In the markets you will never see scallops in their shells. Because the scallops cannot close their shells tightly, they die soon after being taken from the water. Therefore, commercial fishermen must shuck the scallops immediately at sea and ice them for market.

Scallops are available fresh or frozen, all year round. Naturally, they are best in season—from late summer to mid-fall. Florida produces two scallops: the bay scallop and the calico, both about the same size. Look for these small, tender, creamy pink or tan bay scallops rather than the large firm sea scallops. They should have a mild slightly sweet odor and should be free of liquid. Sea scallops, however, are good to use in salads and creamed dishes. After cooking, slice them in thirds against the grain.

Allow ⅓ pound sea scallops or ¼ pound bay scallops per serving for sautéing or broiling.

It is best to use scallops the same day as you bought them, but you can keep them in the refrigerator for two days.

To Freeze Is A Breeze

To retain their quality, scallops should be frozen raw. Cooked scallops that are frozen lose their moisture, texture and flavor. Wash the scallops well, checking for pieces of shell or sand and pack them tightly together in an airtight moisture-proof container. Thaw in the refrigerator or under cold running water. Raw, frozen scallops keep for three to four months in the freezer.

Quick And Easy

Never overcook scallops if you want to retain the natural tenderness, succulence and flavor. Bay scallops should be poached only two minutes, sautéed one to two minutes or baked five to eight minutes. Sea scallops should be poached only four minutes, sautéed two to three minutes, or baked five to eight minutes.

SPICY CEVICHE

1	lb. scallops (if sea scallops, cut each scallop in ⅓" cubes)
½	cup olive oil
½	cup vegetable oil
¼	cup fresh coriander leaves, or 2 teaspoons cracked coriander seeds
½	cup black olives
1½	cups minced Spanish onions
⅔	cup lime juice
3	cloves garlic, minced
2	bay leaves
	freshly ground black pepper to taste
1	pinch of salt
3	drops Tabasco sauce
½	cup finely chopped celery
½	cup finely chopped fresh scallions

1. Place scallops or cubed fish in a shallow glass bowl.
2. Blend olive oil, vegetable oil, and coriander leaves. (If using coriander seeds, cook seeds in a portion of the oil for 5 minutes and add to the remaining oil.)
3. Combine oil mixture with olives, onions, lime juice, garlic, and bay leaves.
4. Pour marinade over fish.
5. Sprinkle with pepper and salt. Add Tabasco and chopped celery.
6. Cover bowl and chill fish for 24 hours.
7. Serve cold on a bed of lettuce with some of the marinade. Sprinkle with fresh scallions.

Serves: 8 appetizers
Preparation: 10 minutes (plus 24 hours for chilling)

"Try this as a tantalizing first course. Fillet of sole, cut in ⅓-inch cubes is a good substitute."

SCALLOPS SINGAPORE

2 tablespoons peanut oil
¼ teaspoon salt
¼ teaspoon Accent
10 oz. bay scallops
1" sliced ginger, peeled, smashed and chopped
8 large mushrooms, sliced in thirds
½ tablespoon sherry
½ cup chicken broth
1 scallion, trimmed and shredded
1 tablespoon Oriental oyster sauce (available in groceries or import food stores)
1 tablespoon cornstarch

1. Heat peanut oil in a wok or large skillet over medium high heat. Add salt and Accent.
2. Add scallops and ginger and stir briefly.
3. Add mushrooms and sherry.
4. Stir constantly while adding chicken broth, oyster sauce and scallion. Stir and gradually add cornstarch until sauce starts to thicken. Serve immediately.

Serves: 2
Preparation: 10 minutes
Cooking: 10 minutes

"This can be served as an appetizer or a main course, as it is easy to double or triple the recipe. Substitute soy sauce if oyster sauce is not available."

RAIMONDO'S ARTICHOKES JULANN WITH SCALLOPS

—ARTICHOKES—

4   small artichokes
1   cup white wine
    juice from 2 lemons
    water

1. Put artichokes in a large pot with the wine and lemon juice. Add enough water to cover the artichokes. Cover and blanch until done—about 30 minutes. Remove artichokes and cool.
2. Cut out the centers of the artichokes. They will be stuffed later with the scallops.

—SCALLOPS—

12 oz. of bay scallops
1   cup champagne
2   shallots, finely chopped
    touch of cayenne pepper
    pinch of salt

1. Wash the scallops well and dry. Blanch them in a combination of champagne, shallots, cayenne pepper and salt.
2. Before they are completely cooked, remove the scallops and let cool.
3. Reduce* the champagne mixture to an essence (about a tablespoon). Let cool.

—SAUCE—

1   teaspoon dry English mustard
    juice from 1 lemon
2   egg yolks
1   cup very fine olive oil
2   whole pimientos, pureed in blender or food processor
    Beluga caviar
    chopped parsley
    champagne or wine

163

1. Remove the champagne essence from above and put into a mixing bowl.
2. Add mustard, lemon juice and the egg yolks and whisk together.
3. Add the olive oil, a few drops at a time, mixing constantly, keeping the mixture thick and smooth (same procedure as for making mayonnaise).
4. Add and stir in the pimientos.
5. Fold the scallops into the sauce carefully.
6. Fill the artichoke centers with the sauced scallops. Top with caviar.
7. To the remaining sauce, add enough chopped parsley to color it green. Thin with a little wine or champagne so that it will nap easily.
8. To serve, turn outside leaves of the artichoke down and pour the green sauce around the artichoke, over the turned-down leaves.

*See glossary

Serves: 4 as an appetizer
Preparation: 30 to 45 minutes
Cooking: 45 minutes

"This is an extremely attractive dish to serve. The color combination of the artichoke, caviar and the sauces creates a dramatic first course."

SCALLOP TERRINE

1½ lbs. fresh baby bay scallops
3 cups heavy whipping cream
6 whole eggs
¼ lb. fresh clean spinach
½ teaspoon saffron
1 cup white wine
salt and pepper

1. Warm 1 cup heavy cream and stir in saffron until mixture is bright yellow. Let cool.
2. In a food processor, mix until smooth: ½ lb. scallops, 2 eggs, 1 cup heavy cream, ⅓ cup white wine, salt and pepper. Remove and put aside in refrigerator.
3. Clean bowl for processor and mix until smooth: ½ lb. scallops, 2 eggs, 1 cup heavy cream, ¼ lb. spinach, ⅓ cup white wine, salt and pepper.
4. Remove mixture and put aside in refrigerator.
5. Clean bowl for processor and mix until smooth: ½ lb. scallops, 2 eggs, saffron-cream infusion, ⅓ cup white wine, salt and pepper.
6. Remove from bowl and refrigerate.
7. In a terrine, layer as follows: white/green/yellow/green/white.
8. Bake in water bath at 350°F. for 1 hour. Let cool overnight.

Serves: 4 to 6
Preparation: 20 minutes (plus chilling overnight)
Cooking: 1 hour

"Easy recipe . . . great results. Chef Tom Klauber's original . . . you must try it!"

SCALLOPS MOUSSELINE

2   lbs. scallops
2   tablespoons butter
     salt and pepper
2   teaspoons lemon juice
2   tablespoons heavy cream,
     whipped
3-4 tablespoons hollandaise*

1. Sauté the scallops in 2 tablespoons butter. Use an oven-proof pan.
2. When almost done, add salt, pepper and lemon juice.
3. Fold the whipped cream into the hollandaise and spread over the scallops.
4. Put under the broiler until golden.

*See glossary

Serves: 4 to 6
Preparation: 10 minutes
Cooking: 5 minutes

"Use a good hollandaise sauce in this recipe, as it is a dominant (but not overpowering) part of this recipe. Next time you have extra hollandaise, freeze it in 'dollops.' Heat over a double boiler, whisking all the time before using it in a recipe. This dish is perfect for luncheon, a light supper or as an elegant appetizer."

SCALLOPS
IN GREEN SAUCE

1½ pounds scallops
2 cups sliced mushrooms
1 cup dry white wine
1½ teaspoons salt
1 cup watercress leaves
2 cups spinach leaves
(4 oz. greens in all)

1. Place scallops, mushrooms, wine and salt in saucepan over medium heat until it almost comes to a boil. Scallops will whiten but barely cook through. Stir occasionally.
2. Strain liquid into another pot. Cover scallops to prevent drying out.
3. Add greens to liquid in the pan, stir and bring to a boil. Greens should be just wilted.
4. Remove with a slotted spoon into food processor or food mill.
5. Puree.
6. Reduce* liquid to ½ cup and put into processor with greens. Blend until smooth.

—SAUCE FOR SCALLOPS—
2 egg yolks
2 tablespoons cream
¼ teaspoon white pepper
1 cup vegetable oil or ½ olive oil, ½ peanut oil

1. Add yolks, cream, and white pepper to greens in processor.
2. Gradually add oil and process.
3. Serve scallops in shells with sauce.

*See glossary

Serves: 4 as appetizer
Preparation: 15 minutes
Cooking: 15 to 20 minutes (depends on how long it takes to reduce juices)

"The remaining sauce would be good served over pasta."

PADELLE
REALE NATALIA
(Fresh Sea Scallops)

10	oz. fresh scallops
	seasoned flour
¼	cup olive oil
1	clove garlic, crushed
	pinch of salt
	pinch of crushed red pepper
¼	cup white wine (or to taste)
6	oz. peeled plum tomatoes, chopped

1. Wash the scallops. Drain and pat dry.
2. Dip the scallops in the seasoned flour (salt, pepper).
3. Pour the olive oil into a frying pan and heat.
4. When the oil is very hot, add the scallops and the garlic.
5. When the scallops are golden brown, add the salt, red pepper, wine and tomatoes.
6. Simmer for 4 to 5 minutes. Taste for seasoning.

Serves: 2
Preparation: 10 minutes
Cooking: 4 to 5 minutes

"Tasty and simple to prepare. You might serve it over rice or pasta."

MUSSEL MAN

Mussels

Epicures' Delight

In Europe, mussels have been popular for centuries. In fact, many European epicures prefer them to any other shellfish. The demand is so great there that for many years mussels have been propagated to augment the natural supply. In the United States, however, mussels are probably one of the greatest unused seafood resources. They are found in the "wild" form on just about all seacoasts.

This delicate bivalve has a thin, blue-black shell, measuring two to three inches long, with a deep violet color inside. They spin a very strong silken black thread called "byssus" or "beard" to anchor themselves to underwater objects. The best mussels are harvested from colder waters, although they are found in all the world's oceans.

Versatility Plus

Mussels can be cooked in a multitude of ways: broiled, fried, simmered, scalloped, added to soups or omelets, smoked, curried, mariniere, as fritters, as a stuffing, with spaghetti, stewed, in a bouillabaisse or as a garnish to fish dishes. They can be steamed, removed from their shells, breaded, and served much like oysters or clams. Or they can be served with a sauce, shell and all.

Take Care!

They are susceptible to water pollution because, like other bivalves, they continuously draw sea water through their siphons to obtain nourishment and strain everything, including pollutants, from it. Those mussels which are propagated are done so under suitably strict conditions. They are plump, delicious, and safe. Because mussel culture requires less time and effort than oysters do, they are usually cheaper than oysters.

No mussels are taken commercially in Florida. They are generally too small and too few to make it worth while. The fresh mussels sold in Florida markets are shipped from Puget Sound or New England.

Eat 'Em Fast!

Mussels can be purchased in the shell alive or canned in either brine, a hot barbeque sauce, or smoked. The shells of the fresh live ones should be tightly closed. If there is a gap between the shells, tap the mussel, and if alive it should close. To check for "mudders," try to slide two halves of the shell across each other. If they budge, the shells may be filled with mud.

Mussels are very perishable, so they should be cooked and eaten the same day. Buy about five pounds of the choicest jumbo live ones for six servings, or one to two dozen per person for a main dish.

Clean With "Muscle"

While holding the mussel under cold running water, scrub with a stiff brush to remove the mud on the outer shell and most, if not all, of the "beard" that protrudes from the edges. Place them in a pot, cover with cold tap water, and let stand for two hours. Live mussels will drop to the bottom. Dead ones will float to the surface. Discard the dead mussels.

To open, place a pan on the table to catch the liquid which you will want to save for sauce. Hold the scrubbed mussel over the pan. Insert a knife between the shells in the bearded area and run a blade around the edge, working first toward the beard end. There is little skill necessary to do this as the shells are so thin. Remove the meat, trim away any remaining whiskers, and place the meat in a separate dish from the liquid. Strain the liquid through two layers of cheesecloth to remove any sand or shells.

Steam 'N Serve

Mussels cook very quickly. They are done just as soon as they have opened their shells.

To steam, put one inch of water into a pot. Add salt and bring to a boil. Slide cleaned, unshelled mussels gently into the pot. Cover and simmer three minutes or less—just until they open. Remove mussels carefully so as not to lose the liquid inside the shells. Let cool just until you can handle them. Pour the liquid from the shells through a cheesecloth to save for sauce. Remove the shell, trim whiskers, and taste for doneness. If they are not quite done, you can return them to the pot for one to three minutes.

Mussels can be used in just about any dish calling for clams or oysters. And don't throw away the shells. You may want to use them as mussel serving dishes.

171

MOULES MARINIÈRE

24-48 mussels (depending on size and
     appetite)
1   stick of butter
1½-2 onions, finely chopped
     basil and marjoram to taste
   4 cloves garlic, minced
   2 cups white wine
   1 cup heavy cream

1. Scrub the mussels and remove the beards. Discard any
   that are already open.
2. In a large, heavy-based pan, melt the butter.
3. Add the onions, herbs, and garlic, and cook over medium
   heat until the onions are translucent.
4. Add the mussels to the pan. Cover tightly and turn the heat
   up. Shake the pan during the cooking process so that all
   the mussels get equal heat and don't stick. Cook just until
   all the mussels are open (check in about 30 seconds).
5. Remove the lid and pour in the wine and the cream.
6. Reduce the heat and cook for 2 to 3 minutes, shaking the
   pan gently so that the sauce is mixed with the mussels.
7. To serve, ladle the mussels and sauce into 4 individual
   serving bowls. Or you may serve them "family style" from 1
   large serving dish, letting everyone take their mussels
   from the community dish. Have a separate dish for the
   shells.

Serves: 4
Preparation: 30 minutes (including cleaning of mussels)
Cooking: 15 minutes

*"The chef says you can adjust the seasonings to your own
taste. Serve this dish with lots of crusty French bread to
soak up the delicious sauce. This is a classic dish in
France and Belgium where nearly every restaurant worth
its salt has it on the menu!"*

MOULES POULETTE
(Mussels in Cream Sauce)

4	lbs. fresh mussels (well-cleaned and scrubbed to remove all sand)
2	cups water
2	cups white wine
	juice of 1 lemon
2	shallots, chopped
¼	lb. butter
1	cup flour
3	egg yolks
8	oz. heavy cream
	salt and pepper to taste
1	bunch parsley, chopped

1. Place the mussels in a large pot with water, wine and lemon juice. Steam 7 to 8 minutes or until shells open. Reserve liquid.
2. Place each mussel on shell half. Arrange on large heat-proof platter or individual plates.
3. Strain liquid through a cloth napkin.
4. Sauté shallots in butter. Add flour, stirring constantly with a whisk until smooth. Add reserved liquid. Stir until medium thick.
5. Beat in egg yolks, cream and parsley, stirring. Taste for seasoning.
6. Anoint the mussels with sauce and serve hot.

Serves: 4 as entrée, 8 as appetizer
Preparation: 20 to 30 minutes
Cooking: 8 to 10 minutes

"If you're a mussel lover, or even if you're not, you'll enjoy this. Serve very hot!"

Notes

KING
CONCH

Conch

Big And Beautiful

Most anyone who has ever walked on a beach has seen a conch—a beautiful, spiral-shaped shellfish. Conch shells have been used for decoration, to "listen to the sea," and as horns. They have even been ground up to make porcelain and burnt to make lime. On occasion, pearls have been found in the Queen Conch which is native to the Bahamas.

Warm Water Winner

Conch (pronounced "conk") are particularly abundant year round in the Key West area of Florida—so much so that the natives of Key West are often referred to as "conchs."

Shallow water, coral reefs and rocks are good places to hunt for conch. Look for smaller ones as they are the most tender. To test if a conch is still alive (don't take it for food if it is not) tap the "trapdoor." If it closes, the conch is alive. There is a limit to how many one can gather or have at the same time, so be sure to check with someone in the know.

Conch can be purchased frozen (cooked, partially cooked, or uncooked), canned (cooked), by the piece or by the pound. Fresh conch should be used within 24 hours. Frozen conch should be used within a week. Figure on two conch per person or one pound for six people when used as part of a recipe.

A Task To Tenderize

There are several ways to deal with live conch, but there are two common denominators no matter what you do—uncooked conch must be tenderized (either with lime juice or banging with the side of a plate) and the tough leathery skin must be peeled off. To remove the meat from the conch you should knock the bulging side with a hammer to help break the shell. Insert a knife and twist it around until you feel the muscle being severed. Grab whatever is sticking out and pull hard. Then cut away the stomach and tail and proceed with removing the skin.

Conch can be used for fritters, stews, soups and chowders. Be adventurous—it's a taste you won't soon forget.

176

PAPPAS' MARINATED CONCH

5	lbs. conch, out of shell
1	qt. lemon juice
2	large white onions, chopped
1	bunch celery, chopped
3	tablespoons white pepper
3	tablespoons salt
4	limes, squeezed
4	oz. vegetable oil

1. Clean and tenderize the conch and then cut into small pieces.
2. Combine all ingredients in a glass bowl.
3. Cover and chill for at least 4 hours before serving.

Serves: 10 to 20
Preparation: 20 minutes (plus time for tenderizing and chilling)

"Even though the conch is cut into small pieces, you CANNOT skip the tenderizing process. This makes a good appetizer or part of an interesting buffet."

SIPLE'S
MARINATED CONCH
(Make 30 days before serving)

```
5    lbs. conch, cleaned
2½   cups cider vinegar
¼    cup salt
¾    cup olive oil
12   cloves garlic
     feta cheese
     Greek olives
     Salonika peppers
```

We have taken the liberty of quoting Siple's delightful directions verbatim.

1. First pound conch. This is the secret to making it edible. Use the pointed side of a meat hammer. Pound unmercifully 'til the muscle portion is riddled with holes. Give special attention to the thicker portion of the muscle.
2. After your arm recovers from the pounding, boil a gallon of water. Add salt and conch. Cover and lower heat to maintain a steady boil. Allow to cook for 40 minutes, moving conch around occasionally.
3. Remove and cool. Place the cooked conch into sterilized glass jars.
4. Add vinegar, olive oil and water. Peel and bruise 12 cloves of garlic and drop in. Cover tightly. Shake well to mix. Set in refrigerator for at least 30 days. Shake one time a week— DO NOT GET IMPATIENT. It will be ready in 30 days, no less.
5. Cut in julienne* strips when ready. Serve with the feta, olives and peppers.

*See glossary

Serves: a lot of people
Preparation: as long as it takes to tenderize the conch
Cooking: 40 minutes

"Serve as an appetizer. Remember: don't cheat; wait the 30 days . . . it's worth it."

BAHAMIAN CRACKED CONCH

1	4 to 6-oz. conch steak (well tenderized)
1	cup herbed flour* for dredging
4	eggs
1	cup milk
3	teaspoons clarified butter*
2	tablespoons lime juice (Key limes preferred)

*Flour with salt, pepper, thyme, pinch baking powder

1. Tenderize conch steak with hammer (kitchen type) until the conch doubles in size. This will take at least 10 minutes.
2. Dredge steak in herbed flour.
3. Dip in egg wash made by mixing 4 eggs with 1 cup milk.
4. Dredge back in flour while heating butter.
5. Sauté conch in butter for 30 seconds over high heat. Turn. Lower heat. Add Key lime juice and serve.

*See glossary

Serves: 1
Preparation: 15 minutes
Cooking: 5 minutes

"This is heavenly. Enjoy this feast on the porch of the Bagatelle, overlooking the festivities of Duval Street!"

CRACKED CONCH FOR TWO

4	large conch
1	egg, beaten
	flour
	salt and pepper
	vegetable oil

1. Remove meat from shells.
2. Pound until tender (about 10 minutes).
3. Flip conch in egg. Roll in flour seasoned with salt and pepper.
4. Fry in oil at low heat until brown on both sides.

Serves: 2
Preparation: 20 minutes
Cooking: 20 minutes

"An easy way to prepare conch."

KEY WEST
CONCH SALAD
(Marinate Ahead)

1	cucumber, peeled and seeded
1	lb. conch
½	red onion
½	red pepper
½	cup cilantro (or Chinese parsley or coriander)
	juice of six limes
1	cup olive oil
1	level teaspoon leaf oregano
1	level teaspoon sugar
½	level teaspoon salt
½	level teaspoon ground black pepper

1. Chop conch in ⅛-inch pieces, cover with lime juice. Marinate for 24 hours.
2. Drain.
3. Chop onions, cucumbers, cilantro and bell pepper finely.
4. Combine all ingredients.
5. Refrigerate for 24 hours.

Serves: 4
Preparation: 10 minutes (plus 48 hours to marinate and refrigerate)

"Enjoy this at home or overlooking the beautiful water at the Pier House in Key West."

CONCH FRITTERS

2 cups self-rising flour
2 cups conch, tenderized
and finely chopped
1 large onion, diced
1 green pepper, diced
salt and pepper
2 dashes Tabasco sauce
2 eggs, lightly beaten
¾ cup (approximately) milk

1. Combine all of the above ingredients with enough milk for the mixture to hold its shape.
2. Form into fritters and fry in 350°F. oil until golden.
3. Drain on paper towels and serve with the sauce below (or the sauce of your choice).

—HOT SAUCE—

24 oz. catsup
¼ cup Worcestershire sauce
3 datil (or very hot peppers), finely chopped

1. Combine all of the ingredients. Makes 1 quart and will keep in a covered glass jar for a week or two.

Serves: 4 to 6
Preparation: 30 minutes
Cooking: 20 minutes (approximately)

"Make the sauce a few hours in advance so it can mellow. Even though the conch is finely chopped (we did it in a food processor), you MUST tenderize it first. The sauce can be used for ribs or shrimp."

Big
MacGator

Alligator

Makes A Snappy Dish

Alligators abound in Florida—in lakes, canals, drainage ditches, swamps—almost anywhere there is "fresh" water. But *don't* try to catch one yourself. If you don't get bitten (or eaten) you might get arrested! Alligators are protected by law in Florida.

The flavor is similar to chicken and can be handled like veal. The meat from the loin is considered by many to be the best.

Commercial alligator farming in Florida is increasing by leaps and bounds. However, you may not purchase the meat for home preparation. Farmers sell directly to the restaurants and allotments are carefully screened.

You must try this dish—"Florida Crackers" (those born and raised here) list alligator among their favorites. Try it at one of the many Florida restaurants that serve it several different ways.

Turtle

Turtle—A Taste Treat

At this writing, turtle, also known as terrapin or tortoise, can probably only be purchased canned unless you can find a dealer who has access to a turtle farm. At one time there was a great deal of commercial turtle fishing done in Key West. However, in most places it is now illegal to catch marine turtles (or even touch their eggs that you might stumble across on the beach).

Turtle fanciers say that the greenish meat from the tops of the shell is considered to be the tastiest. The meat is used mainly for soup and for stews and even "turtleburgers."

Because of all the restrictions placed on catching turtles we will assume that you have purchased your turtle meat at the store so we will not go into how to clean. It can be enjoyed many ways—try it sautéed with mushrooms, onions, and green peppers!

184

Eel

Slippery But Succulent

Most North Americans look upon eel with less than gustatory glee. But for those who have tried eel they find it really is delicious. Eel is a true member of the fish family and can be caught in all seasons. There are eel in creeks, sounds, bays, and rivers. Atlantic eel are spawned in the Sargasso Sea and then travel on to their various destinations. Because the parent eel dies after spawning, commercial fishermen will try to catch them as they migrate downstream to lay their eggs.

Catch Them Yourself

If you want to catch eel yourself, you can spear them at night using underwater lights. Consult with a sporting goods store about eel traps, or fish for them using a sinker that will rest on the bottom.

Rich And Fatty

Eel can be purchased in many ethnic neighborhoods, particularly around Christmas time. The meat is rich and fatty and is particularly good smoked or pickled. Eel can also be sautéed or broiled. Figure on a half pound per person and plan to use within one day of purchase (or catch). Eel can be purchased whole, smoked, pickled, or canned.

To Skin An Eel

To skin an eel (and this should be done while they are alive) get friendly with your fish dealer and let him do it, as it is a wretched job. If you are not queasy, there are directions in many cookbooks. First you grab the eel by the neck to keep it still and then—well . . . you get the picture.

Snails

Pokey Vegetarians

Did you know that most of the snails served in restaurants are shorebound creatures? These pokey vegetarians are very close cousins to sea snails or periwinkles and are cooked in the same manner.

Snails found in the markets, either canned or fresh, are literally not your garden variety. At specialized "snail ranches," the snails have been through a lengthy process of fasting, soaking, and rinsing—which takes weeks. Fresh snails found in American markets have been through this purging process. However, they still must be soaked in warm water, boiled in salted water or bouillion and cleaned. That's why we recommend you treat yourself to the canned variety, making it that much easier to feast immediately on the most popular snail dish of all—escargots with garlic butter.

Snails Can Be Habit Forming

The Romans' addiction to snails was such that they pampered the snails with special foods such as spicy soups, bay and wine to pre-season them before cooking.

Fresh snails are commonplace in French markets. The French are very enthusiastic snail eaters and often purchase them already prepared with garlic butter in their shells, ready for heating. Many French, albeit very patient ones, even catch them and put them through the long process previously described.

Easy To Prepare—Easy To Eat

When using the canned variety, put the snails in a colander and pour one quart of warm water or one half cup of wine over them. Drain them and they are ready to prepare with your recipe.

If possible, serve the snails in special heated "escargot" dishes, which are grooved and cupped to capture the delicious snail butter. Use a spring handled holder to pick up the snail shell and remove the snail with a small, closely tined fork. Assuredly addictive!

Frog Legs

Finding The Fabulous Frog

Frogs are amphibians who spend most of their time in and around water—particularly marshes, ponds, and lakes. If you want to catch frogs for eating, don't go hunting in the winter months as they usually hibernate until spring when the females lay their eggs. Look for bullfrogs (quite large), green or spring frogs (medium), or the leopard frogs as these three are the most edible species in the United States. Catch the frogs with your bare hands if you are quick and quiet or mesmerize them with a flashlight and capture them with a net. In any case, keep the frogs in a well-ventilated enclosure with a tight top.

Luckily, for the less adventuresome, edible frogs are commercially grown (and sold in fish markets all over) in Florida, Louisiana, California and the midwest. Also available are frozen legs imported from Japan.

I've Got The Frog, Now What?

Frogs must be killed before skinning and cooking. Then, use a pair of scissors to cut the frogs legs as close to their body as possible, making sure that the legs are still intact. Skinning is done from top to bottom, and it is easier to do if you chill the frogs legs. As a rule, the legs are the only part of the frog that are eaten.

Frogs legs should be white (after skinning) for the best flavor and texture. Before you use the legs for any recipe, soak them for at least two hours in cold milk, water, or even beer. The legs can be sautéed, fried, or poached. Because the legs are so fragile, use two large spatulas to turn them while cooking. Six small (the most succulent) or three medium pair will serve one person.

If you haven't tried frogs legs, be adventurous . . . they're a most enjoyable delicacy.

Squid

Inside Out Shellfish

Squid (well known as calamari on Italian menus) are true mollusks although they don't look like it, as squid lack an outer shell.

Squid are elongated in shape and swim by jetting water through their bodies. Squid can swim forwards or backwards as the occasion demands. Commercial fishing for squid has been on the increase in North America as consumer acceptance and demand have increased. The fishermen detect them with echo sounders during the day and go after them when they rise to the surface at night.

Worth The Trouble To Find

Squid can be purchased fresh or frozen. Canned are available but are hard to find. Fresh squid should be creamy in color with red flecks. To clean, either have your fish dealer do it or consult *Romagnolis' Table* for step-by-step photographs. Fresh cleaned squid will last two days in the refrigerator, frozen, one month in the freezer.

Weight-Watching Delight

Squid is high in protein, low in calories and is a good buy as almost all of it is edible. (Two pounds whole will yield 1½ pounds cleaned.) Before cooking, squid must be tenderized. It can be fried, stewed, sautéed or poached, stir-fried or deep fried. Just don't overcook as it tends to become quite rubbery. Enjoy! It could be habit forming.

Octopus

Decidedly Different

Octopi are closely related to the smaller squid but are rarely found in the Atlantic. If you should happen to catch an octopus (the smaller the better) knock it over the head to stun or kill it. Remove the eyes, suckers, ink sack, and mouth and then wash in several changes of water. Blanch, then remove the skin. Better yet, buy it frozen or ask the fish store to do the cleaning.

To tenderize the octopus—beat it, literally, with a mallet or against the side of a table. Once tenderized, octopus should be cut in one-inch pieces before cooking. It can be stewed, fried, or sautéed according to your favorite recipe. A delight that must be tried.

SILAS DENT'S ALLIGATOR

1 lb. alligator*
4 whole eggs
16 oz. beer
1 tablespoon salt
1 tablespoon pepper
1 tablespoon granulated garlic
8 oz. milk
seasoned self-rising flour
(with salt, pepper, granulated
garlic)
vegetable oil for frying

1. Cut the alligator meat with the grain into 1-inch strips. Pound to tenderize.
2. Mix the eggs, beer, salt, pepper, and granulated garlic in a glass dish or bowl. Add the alligator meat and marinate for 24 hours in the refrigerator.
3. Mix the flour with the salt, pepper, and granulated garlic. Dip the alligator pieces into the flour.
4. Heat the oil to 350°F. and fry the strips, moving them around so that they don't stick. It will take about 1 minute to cook. Serve hot.

*Alligators are protected by law in Florida and are not available for purchase. Enjoy this at Silas Dent's or at one of the many Florida eateries.

Serves: 4
Preparation: 20 minutes (plus 24 hours for marinating)
Cooking: 5 minutes

"This is such a delicious and popular dish that Silas Dent's cooks 2,000 pounds of alligator a year for their customers."

FRIED ALLIGATOR

6   oz. alligator meat
    ice water
    salt and pepper to taste
    flour for dredging
    vegetable oil

1. Cut alligator meat into small, finger-sized pieces.
2. Soak the meat in ice water for about 1 hour.
3. Drain. Season to taste with salt and pepper. Fluff in flour.
4. Deep fry until done (about 5 minutes) at 340°F.

Serves: 1
Preparation: 10 minutes (1 hour for soaking)
Cooking: 5 minutes

"Enjoy at The Yearling. You won't be afraid to get near this alligator!"

GATOR BURGER

2-2½lbs. gator meat
¼   lb. lean, mild Italian sausage in
     bulk form
1-2 eggs
½   cup bread crumbs
     salt, pepper, garlic, onion salt,
     Accent to taste.

1. Grind gator meat, normally a tough, fine and fat-free meat. Add sausage to hold meat together.
2. Work in eggs, bread crumbs, and seasonings to taste. Mix thoroughly.
3. Make patties and grill, preferably on a flat surface indoors. Turn carefully with a spatula to avoid crumbling. Serve on a roll and sink *your* teeth into the gator!

Serves: 4 to 6
Preparation: 15 minutes
Cooking: 15 to 20 minutes

"Not your everyday kind of ordinary burger—delicious"

ANGULAS
DE AGUINAGA
(Baby eel)

10	cloves of garlic, sliced
10	oz. fresh baby eel (canned baby eel can be substituted)
	pinch of fresh chopped parsley
	pinch of crushed red pepper
	few drops of sherry
½	cup olive oil
	salt to taste

1. Sauté the garlic in very hot olive oil until golden brown.
2. Add the eel, parsley and red pepper and cook until eel is tender (about 2 to 3 minutes).
3. Stir in the wine and cook for another minute.
4. Serve very, very hot, either in the same dish it was cooked in or in very hot individual serving plates.

Serves: 2
Preparation: 10 minutes
Cooking: 4 minutes

"This appetizer is a true delicacy. Baby eels are tiny—only about 2 inches long—white and very thin. Fresh ones are hard to find, but gourmet and specialty shops occasionally carry them in cans. If you do find them in the market, grab them. You now have the perfect recipe for preparing them!"

FRIED SOFT SHELL TURTLE

> 2   lbs. soft shell turtle* meat
> ice water
> flour
> oil for frying

1. Cut meat into 3- or 4-ounce pieces
2. Soak in ice water for a few minutes
3. Fluff in flour.
4. Fry in heavy iron skillet until done (about 20 to 25 minutes), turning over once.

*In many places it is illegal to catch marine turtles. (Consult your local county.)

Serves: 4
Preparation: 10 minutes
Cooking: 20 to 25 minutes

"This is a great treat at the Yearling—be sure to visit the house of Marjorie Kinnan Rawlings, next door, author of 'The Yearling,' to top off a delightful visit."

FROG LEGS PROVENÇALE

¼	lb. butter, lightly salted
3	large cloves garlic, chopped
12	large fresh mushrooms
½	teaspoon basil, fresh if possible
	freshly ground pepper to taste
12	large pairs frog legs
1	large ripe tomato, chopped
⅓	cup Madeira wine
	juice from ½ lemon
	Parmesan, freshly grated
	scallions, chopped

1. Melt butter over low heat—very slowly—in large skillet.
2. Sauté garlic until edges begin to brown. DO NOT BROWN BUTTER.
3. Add mushrooms and sauté 3 to 4 minutes, turning with wooden spoon frequently.
4. Add basil and pepper.
5. Place frog legs in skillet.
6. Add tomatoes and push pieces of tomato into butter.
7. Increase heat and let simmer rapidly for 2 to 3 minutes.
8. Add wine and lemon juice.
9. Turn frog legs over, turning carefully to ensure they remain whole.
10. Cover skillet and reduce heat. Simmer 8 to 10 minutes. DO NOT OVERCOOK.
11. Carefully remove frog legs with tongs and place on serving platter.
12. Cover with gravy remaining in skillet and sprinkle with fresh Parmesan. Garnish with chopped scallions.

Serves: 4
Preparation: 10 minutes
Cooking: 20 minutes

"Enjoy your frog legs with a view at Frogs Landing."

PICKLED OCTOPUS

5 lbs. octopus
1 qt. lemon juice
2 cloves garlic, finely chopped
1 qt. white vinegar
3 tablespoons salt
3 tablespoons black pepper
3 teaspoons oregano
4 oz. water

1. Clean octopus. Skin and boil (or vice-versa) and then chop into small pieces.
2. Mix all ingredients in a glass bowl.
3. Cover and chill for 4 to 6 hours before serving.

Serves: 10 to 20
Preparation: 30 minutes (plus time for chilling)
Cooking: Depends upon how tender the octopus is

"Serve this as a prelude to an Italian or Greek dinner."

SQUID RINGS
(Allow 2 to 3 hours to marinate)

2   lbs. squid*

—MARINADE—
juice of 3 Key limes
(may substitute limes)
3   cloves of garlic, crushed
     and chopped fine
½   teaspoon freshly ground
     black pepper

1. Clean squid*
2. Cut in to ½-inch rings. Mix with marinade ingredients and marinate 2 to 3 hours.

—BATTER—
2   eggs
1   cup milk
1   cup flour
1   lb. fine cracker meal

1. Prepare an egg wash (eggs and milk mixed).
2. Dust squid with flour, dip in egg wash then in cracker meal.
3. Refrigerate 1 hour for breading to set.
4. Deep fry to a golden brown.

*To clean squid, remove the spiney translucent portion and then pull head and legs from the envelope-like covering. Peel skin from the body and cut across the head above the eyes.

Serves: 4 to 6
Preparation: Marinate 2 to 3 hours, refrigerate 1 hour
Cooking: 5 to 10 minutes

"Nice consistency! The flavor is unusual—a popular dish at the Half Shell!"

SQUID
SAUTÉED IN GARLIC

	flour
	salt and pepper
1	lb. squid, cleaned, tenderized and sliced in 1" rounds
¼	cup butter
3	scallions, chopped
1	tablespoon chopped chives
2	cloves garlic, finely chopped
2	oz. white wine

1. Combine flour, salt, and pepper.
2. Lightly flour the squid.
3. Melt butter and add scallions, chives and garlic.
4. Sauté until garlic is golden.
5. Add squid and sauté for 5 to 7 minutes or until squid is done.
6. Just before the squid is finished, add the wine and stir.

Serves: 2
Preparation: 15 minutes
Cooking: 10 minutes

"A spicy and quite delicious appetizer."

ESCARGOTS EMILE

Garlic Butter (see below)
24   escargots (snails) and shells
(available canned)

—GARLIC BUTTER—
¾   lb. lightly salted butter, softened
1   teaspoon Italian seasoning
5   cloves garlic, minced (more for "garlicaholics")
3   oz. white wine
pinch of salt
⅓   teaspoon black pepper
2   teaspoons flour
1   oz. brandy

1. Cream the butter.
2. Add the remaining ingredients (except the snails and shells) and mix well.
3. Refrigerate and then bring to room temperature before using.
4. When ready to cook snails: Put a snail and then ¼ teaspoon of garlic butter in each shell.
5. Put on escargot plate (or baking dish) and bake in a 425°F. oven for 15 minutes.

Serves: 4
Preparation: 5 minutes
Cooking: 15 minutes

"You must have some crusty bread to sop up the sauce (our favorite part of snails). If you are an escargot fanatic, make a dozen of these just for yourself. Save and thoroughly wash the shells so that next time you can purchase just the snails without the shells.

SNAILS IN BRIOCHE

1	brioche with the top removed
5	snails
2	teaspoons butter
¼	teaspoon shallots
⅛	teaspoon minced garlic
⅓	cup Burgundy (red wine)
1	cup vin rouge*

1. Scoop out a small amount of the brioche.
2. Sauté the snails, shallots, and garlic until the snails are cooked through. Remove from pan.
3. Add the Burgundy and reduce* by half.
4. Add 1 cup vin rouge and bring to a boil.
5. Put the snails in the brioche (which you have warmed) and pour the sauce over the snails. Place the cap on the brioche and serve immediately.

*See glossary

Serves: 1
Preparation: 5 minutes
Cooking: 15 minutes

"The brioche can be purchased in many bakeries or supermarkets or you can make your own. What an elegant combination!"

LONE
SHARK

Shark

You just *think* that you haven't eaten shark before, but chances are you have without even knowing it. Until it was outlawed, many fish stores (and restaurants) offered shark as swordfish, halibut, flounder, and probably other species. Even today you have every right to eye with great suspicion perfectly formed, perfectly lined up rows of "scallops."

You Too Can Love A Shark

Americans are now discarding their prejudice against shark and discovering what Europeans, Africans, and Orientals have known for years—shark is an abundant, highly edible, nutritious and low calorie fish with a lovely lack of bones. The meat is light with only a moderately "fishy" flavor. It can be purchased fresh or frozen. Shark can be grilled, poached, broiled, baked, or fried. It lends itself to most swordfish recipes.

Down To The Docks

To get the freshest shark go to the shark tournaments and wait for the contestants to return. Once the entries have been weighed, you'll probably see marine biologists, restaurateurs, and housewives vying with each other to purchase the shark.

Tender Loving Care

If you do catch a shark or buy it from the dock there are certain things to do before cooking. Soak the shark meat in ice water with lemon juice or cider vinegar. This will help to firm up the meat and help to get rid of any ammonia. If you don't use the shark within 24 hours, freeze it.

We suggest that the first few times you try shark fishing, you go with a seasoned expert. Shark fishing just isn't the same as going after mullet!!

KON TIKI SHARK
Á LA SEAPORT

2	lbs. shark fillets (fresh, if possible)
	salt to taste
	flour for dredging
4	eggs, beaten
3-4	teaspoons clarified butter*
	coconut, shredded
½	cup lemon juice, fresh squeezed
	available fresh fruit such as:
	peaches
	apples
	plums
	strawberries
	grapes
	kiwi

1. Slice shark horizontally into ¼" thick fillets.
2. Flatten each fillet with mallet and lightly salt.
3. Dip into flour and then dip into egg batter.
4. Heat clarified butter in skillet to 400°F. It must be very hot.
5. Place fillets in skillet and cook until brown. Turn once and brown other side.
6. Remove fillets from skillet and place on serving platter.
7. Add coconut to the remaining butter in skillet.
8. Wash fruit and slice into ¼" pieces. Pat dry.
9. Place fruit into skillet with juices. Sauté very quickly. Add lemon juice to mixture.
10. Pour sauce over fillets. Garnish and serve with potatoes and fresh vegetables.

*See glossary

Serves: 6 to 8
Preparation: 30 minutes
Cooking: 10 to 15 minutes

"An unusual preparation for an unusual fish. Enjoy this feast at home or at the Seaport Inn."

SILAS DENT'S
SHARK

1½-2 lbs. shark
oil for searing
salt, pepper, granulated garlic
to taste
12   oz. butter
2   oz. lemon juice
rind from 1 lemon
2   teaspoons minced fresh garlic
8   oz. vermouth
16   oz. white wine or water

1. Cut the shark, with the grain, into 4 pieces (approximately 8 or 9 oz. each).
2. Rub the pieces with salt, pepper, and granulated garlic to taste, on both sides.
3. Heat a little oil in a frying pan. When it is very hot, put in the shark and sear it on both sides. Remove from the pan and set aside.
4. Mix together the butter, lemon juice, lemon rind and garlic. Add the vermouth and wine or water and mix well.
5. Put the shark pieces in an oven-proof pan or dish. Pour the butter-wine mixture over the shark.
6. Broil on one side only - about 6 to 8 minutes. Watch the cooking carefully so that the shark does not dry out. (The liquids in the pan will cook the underside).

Serves: 4
Preparation: 20 minutes
Cooking: 6 to 8 minutes

"The seasonings can be adjusted to suit your taste. This is a very simple-to-prepare dish and will probably make a shark fan out of anyone who tastes it!"

SUSHI

Sushi

If you knew sushi like I know sushi . . . you'll love it!
For those of you not familiar with this habit-forming Japanese delicacy (some people actually have "withdrawal" symptoms going without it for too long!) sushi is a combination of raw or cooked seafood or vegetables (called tane) and rice that is formed into decorative, edible packages. The rice is flavored with vinegar and mirin, a sweet rice wine. Sushi is not to be confused with sashimi, thinly-sliced raw fish.
Sushi (pronounced "who-she") preparation began 1500 years ago as a method of preserving fish.
The most popular forms of sushi in the United States are nigiri and makizushi. Nigiri has tane placed on top of small oblong portions of rice. Makizushi means "rolled sushi." A sheet of thin dry nori (seaweed) is laid on a small bamboo mat and spread with rice. The seafood or vegetables are then placed on top, and the seaweed is rolled into a cylinder shape. The roll is then cut into six pieces and served as an appetizer or entrée.
Eating sushi with your fingers is really in! Just take the sushi between your thumb and forefinger and dip it into a soy sauce and wasabi (Japanese horseradish) mixture. By custom, sushi should be eaten in one or two bites.
Garnishes for sushi can include whisper-thin scallion slices and freshly sliced ginger. Sushi preparation and garnishing is truly an art, the sushi chef typically training for six years.
The number of sushi enthusiasts is growing fast as evidenced by the number of sushi "bars" in Florida. For those of you looking for culinary adventure and food with high protein and low calories, this may be *the* cuisine to try.
Okay, everyone to the sushi bar!

Sushi Varieties

There are many varieties of sushi. Listed below is a sampling from the Hyatt Regency in Tampa.

Nigiri Sushi
Raw slices of fish or scallops over vinaigrette rice (sushi rice).

Ebi
   Shrimp, boiled.

Tamago
   Thick omelete sweetened with sugar and mirin, cut in slices and served on rice.

Kappa Maki
   Cucumber-filled rolled sushi.

Toro
   Tuna belly, "white" prime tuna; the fattest cut.

Maguro
   Red meat of tuna (usually the first raw fish that Westerners take to, quite similar to rare steak in taste).

Anago
   A type of sea eel (boiled in seasoned stock then grilled; a thick, sweet sauce is brushed on just before serving).

Nari Sushi
   Bean curd pocket filled with mixture of vinaigrette rice and chopped Oriental relish topped with Kampyo..

Dichi Maki
   Vinaigrette rice, center of avocado, crab meat, pickled daikon strip, rolled in seaweed. This sushi variety is named after the sushi cook at the Hyatt Regency Tampa, Dichi.

GARI
(Pickled Ginger)

½	lb. ginger root
	salt
1	cup rice vinegar
7	tablespoons water
2½	teaspoons sugar
	salt

1. Thoroughly wash, peel, and salt fresh ginger root.
2. Let stand one day.
3. Wash again and place in marinade of rice vinegar, water, and sugar.
4. Marinate ginger for 1 week.
5. Drain, cover and refrigerate. Gari will keep for months.
6. Slice very thin and serve small amount with sushi.

Yield: approximately ½ lb. ginger root
Preparation: 20 minutes (plus salt and 8 days to marinate)

"A most unusually refreshing taste!"

SUSHI RICE

3⅓ cups short-grain rice, washed
4 cups water
3" square giant kelp (konbu)
available at Oriental
food markets.

—DRESSING—

5 tablespoons plus 1 teaspoon
rice vinegar*
5 tablespoons sugar
4 teaspoons sea salt (available at
most gourmet specialty shops)

—TO PREPARE—

1. Place rice in heavy-bottomed, medium-sized pot or rice cooker. Add the water.
2. Clean kelp by wiping with a damp cloth. (More flavors will be released if the kelp is slashed in a few places.) Place kelp on top of rice in water.
3. Cover and heat over medium heat just until the boiling point. When just boiling, remove kelp and discard.
4. Cover tightly, boil over high heat for 2 minutes, then turn heat down to medium and boil for 5 minutes.
5. Reduce heat to very low and cook for 15 minutes, or until all the water has been absorbed.
6. Turn heat off and let stand on burner, with pot lid wrapped in a kitchen towel, for 10 to 15 minutes.
7. Dissolve sugar and salt in the vinegar, stirring over low heat.
8. Force-cool to room temperature by placing hot vinegar mixture in a metal bowl and twirling the bowl in a bath of water and ice.

209

—TO TOSS RICE—

1. Use a flat wooden spoon or proper rice paddle to spread the hot rice in a thin layer in a wide and shallow wooden or plastic bowl. Toss with horizontal, cutting strokes to separate the grains. Use only a sideways cutting motion when mixing.
2. Pour the vinegar mixture generously over the rice. (You may not have to use all the vinegar dressing.) Be careful not to add too much liquid, which will cause the rice to become mushy.
3. As you toss the rice, cool it quickly and thoroughly by fanning it with a folded newspaper or your hand. (It will be easier if you can have someone else standing by to do this.) The tossing and cooling should take about 10 minutes. Taste test to see if the rice is at room temperature.

Note: Vinegared rice should be eaten the same day it is prepared—it does not keep more than 1 day. DO NOT REFRIGERATE! Place the vinegared rice in a container when it has cooled to room temperature, then cover with a damp cloth to keep it from drying out.

*The flavor of sushi rice varies somewhat with the seasons. A little more vinegar may be used in the summer. Adjust the flavor of the rice to suit your taste.

Preparation: 1 hour
Cooking: 30 to 40 minutes
Yields: approximately 10 cups rice

"Be sure to keep rice from drying out, as proper moistness is a must for good sushi!"

KEY WEST ROLL

nori (seaweed, found in Oriental
food markets)
vinegar and water
sushi rice*
sesame seeds
wasabi (Japanese horseradish,
found in Oriental food markets)
crab cake (found in most
seafood stores)
avocado
cucumber

1. Place sheet of nori (seaweed) on a bamboo sushi mat.
   (Available at Oriental food markets.)
2. Moisten hands with vinegar water.
3. Place rice (size of a lemon) in middle of nori. Spread
   evenly from left to right.
4. Sprinkle sesame seeds on rice.
5. Put sheet Saran Wrap over rice mixture. Flip so rice will be
   on bottom, resting on bamboo mat.
6. Spread a dash of wasabi across the middle of the nori.
7. Place 2 small slices of avocado, one piece of crab cake
   and one piece of thinly sliced cucumber across the
   middle of the nori.
8. Starting on edge closest to you, use mat to roll up the
   sushi.
9. Remove roll from bamboo mat.
10. Remove Saran Wrap. Cut the roll in half using wet knife
    dipped in vinegar water. Cut each half into 3 equal
    pieces.
11. Serve with wasabi and pickled ginger.

*See index

Serves: 1 roll serves 1 person
Preparation: 5 minutes

*"This is beautifully done at Kyushu, the sesame seeds
adding a nice flavor to what other sushi bars call
'California Roll'!"*

WASABI
(Japanese horseradish)

1   can powdered wasabi
(available in Oriental food
markets)
water

1. Mix wasabi with small amount of tepid water.
2. Allow to stand for 10 minutes before using.

Yield: depends on amount of powdered wasabi
Preparation: 5 minutes

"Powerful . . . great flavor, it will definitely clean out your sinuses!"

EMMERT

POTPOURRI

OYSTER AND LOBSTER, CUISINE NOUVELLE

4-6	Maine lobsters or Florida lobster tails
12-15	oysters, shucked
1	carrot, julienne*
1	leek, julienne
2	tablespoons butter
4	shallots
1	tablespoon oil
2	oz. brandy
1	bunch parsley (½ chopped, ½ for garnish)
1½	cups whipping cream
	salt and pepper to taste
4	tablespoons butter

1. Parboil lobster tails. Remove meat. Cut in cubes and set aside.
2. Sauté carrots and leeks in 2 tablespoons butter for 2 minutes. Remove from pan.
3. Sauté shallots in oil in same pan for 2 minutes.
4. Add lobster cubes and oysters. Stir until seared. Remove contents from pan.
5. Flambé* residue carefully with brandy. Add chopped parsley and cream. Season with salt and pepper and reduce.*
6. Add 4 tablespoons butter and stir until smooth and creamy.
7. Add lobster and oysters. Simmer 1 minute.
8. To serve, pour on serving plate. Sprinkle julienne vegetables on top. Garnish with parsley sprigs.

*See glossary

Serves: 6
Preparation: 15 minutes
Cooking: 20 minutes

"Very exciting . . . use fresh oysters for the best flavor."

SEAFOOD VENETIAN

8	oz. thick bechamel sauce*
10	oz. fresh snapper fillet
10	oz. shrimp (21 to 25 per lb.)
10	oz. sea scallops
5	oz. king crab leg meat
3	oz. butter
10	oz. mushrooms, sliced
1	clove garlic, minced
5	oz. clam juice
2	oz. white wine
	salt, pepper, lemon juice to taste

1. Prepare the bechamel sauce and keep warm.
2. Remove all the bones from the snapper and cut into 1-ounce pieces.
3. Peel, devein, and butterfly the shrimp.
4. Wash the scallops and pat dry.
5. Pick over the crab carefully for bits of shell.
6. Melt the butter in a large skillet and sauté the snapper, shrimp, and scallops until almost done. Remove from skillet.
7. Into the same skillet, put the mushrooms and garlic and sauté for 1 minute. Then add the clam juice, white wine, and bechamel sauce.
8. Reduce* mixture until thick. Season with salt, pepper and lemon juice to taste.
9. Add the sautéed snapper, shrimp and sea scallops to the sauce. Add the crab and simmer for 2 minutes.
10. Serve over rice pilaf.

*See glossary

Serves: 4
Preparation: 20 minutes
Cooking: 10 minutes

"You're 'gondola' like this one!"

215

CAPTAIN'S SALAD

1	head iceberg lettuce, medium
1	head romaine lettuce, medium
12	oz. fresh lump crab meat or Alaskan king crab meat
12	oz. cooked small shrimp, peeled and deveined
½	cup thinly sliced radishes
2	stalks celery, finely diced
1	medium onion, finely diced
1	medium green pepper, finely diced
½	cup black olive pieces
4	anchovy fillets

1. Wash and tear iceberg and romaine lettuce. Drain well and mix together. Place in a large wooden bowl, peaking slightly in the center.
2. Mentally divide the bowl into 6 equal wedges, like slices of a pie. On opposite wedges place the crab meat and the shrimp, leaving the center of the bowl open for the sliced radishes.
3. In 2 other opposite wedges spread the diced celery and onions. In the last 2 wedges spread the diced green pepper and black olive pieces. Top with anchovy fillets.
4. Present the bowl of salad to your guests and then remove the salad to toss with your favorite dressing.

Serves: 4 to 6
Preparation: 20 minutes

"Great with a Roquefort or oil and vinegar dressing. A perfect summertime treat redolent of the sea."

PÂTÉ NEPTUNE

—CREPES—

½ cup flour
1 egg
¾ cup milk
½ teaspoon salt
2 tablespoons butter

1. Combine flour, egg, milk, salt and 1 tablespoon melted butter to make crepes.
2. Make crepes in butter in a 5-inch crepe pan and set aside.

—FILLING—

¼ lb. spinach
1 lb. boneless skinless salmon
1 lb. scallops
1 lb. boneless skinless halibut
2 cups heavy cream
3 egg whites
¾ teaspoon salt per pound of fish
¼ teaspoon pepper (white) each for scallops and halibut
¼ teaspoon cayenne pepper for salmon

1. Blanch* spinach and cool.
2. Put very cold salmon in food processor. Start motor and add 1 egg white, ¾ cup cream, ¾ teaspoon salt, and ¼ teaspoon cayenne pepper. Process, then remove and put aside.
3. Put very cold scallops in processor. Start motor and add 1 egg white, ¾ cup heavy cream, ¾ teaspoon salt, ¼ teaspoon pepper. Process, then remove and put aside.
4. Put very cold halibut in food processor. Start motor and add 1 egg white; ½ cup heavy cream; cold, drained spinach; ¾ teaspoon salt, and ¼ teaspoon white pepper.
5. Butter a 3½-lb. mold. Line with crêpes.
6. Layer the various colors of the filling in the crêpes; or arrange the fish and spinach so that the colors make a

circle in the center of the mold (this takes practice!). Be sure to work with dry hands or spatula when layering the puree into the mold.

7. Cover with the crepes. Place mold in larger pan with hot water half way up sides of mold.

8. Place in a preheated oven 250°F. Cook almost 2 hours. Temperature in center should reach 160°F.

9. Can be served hot or cold. Usually served cold. Serve with one of the sauces listed below.

—COLD SAUCE #1—

mayonnaise
watercress
spinach
a little sour cream

1. Process all together. Create to your own taste.

—COLD SAUCE #2—

1	large tomato, seeded and coarsely chopped (about 1 cup)
½	teaspoon good paprika
	dash of cayenne
1	teaspoon salt
¼	teaspoon white pepper
1	tablespoon good red wine vinegar
1	egg yolk
1	cup good oil

1. Combine all ingredients except the oil in processor.
2. Blend 30 to 40 seconds until smooth.
3. With motor still running, add oil slowly (about 15 to 20 seconds). Taste for seasonings. If too thick, add 1 to 2 tablespoons lukewarm water until it is a creamy consistency.

*See glossary

Serves: 8 to 10
Preparation: 1 hour, including crêpe-making time
Cooking: 2 hours

"This is a very impressive-looking dish to set before your most sophisticated friends. Keeps for 2 to 3 days in the refrigerator. Take on the boat with you and produce at cocktail time to wow your sailing pals."

TREASURES OF THE SEA

1	lb. bay scallops
	"washwater" from the scallops
3	cups water
1	sprig of parsley
2	bay leaves
½	medium onion, diced
1	stalk celery, diced
½	teaspoon white peppercorns
	salt to taste
4	oz. butter
6	tablespoons flour
½	cup dry white wine
½	cup heavy cream
2	teaspoons lemon juice
	dash of cayenne pepper
8	oz. small shrimp, cooked, peeled and deveined
8	oz. lump crab meat
8	oz. mushrooms, sliced and sautéed in butter
4	oz. finely chopped pimientos
4	large shrimp with tails left on, peeled and deveined
	Parmesan cheese for garnish

1. Wash the scallops in 1 or 2 cups of water and save this "washwater." Strain the "washwater."
2. In a saucepan, put water, parsley, bay leaves, onion,

celery, peppercorns, and salt to taste. Bring to a boil.
3. Add the "washwater" and simmer slowly until a good stock flavor is reached—about 15 to 20 minutes. Strain this court bouillon.
4. Preheat the oven to 400°F.
5. In another saucepan, melt the butter and stir in the flour. When all flour has been absorbed into the butter, add about 2 cups of the court bouillon, stirring constantly. Remove the sauce from the heat and beat vigorously with a wire whisk or electric mixer.
6. Add wine. Beat in the heavy cream, lemon juice, and cayenne. Continue beating until cool.
7. Mix the scallops, small shrimp, crab meat, mushrooms, and pimientos in a large bowl.
8. Divide into 4 casserole dishes. Top each with a large shrimp in the center. Cover with the sauce. Sprinkle with Parmesan cheese.
9. Bake until bubbling—about 10 minutes.

Serves: 4
Preparation: 30 minutes
Cooking: 30 to 40 minutes

"The chef explained that saving the 'washwater' from the scallops is very important. This 'essence of the sea' from the scallops is therefore captured and gives an added flavor to the court bouillon and later to the sauce. Try this and you'll see!"

CASSEROLE OF BAKED EGGPLANT, SHRIMP AND CRAB MEAT

2	medium eggplant, peeled and cut into large dice
2	tablespoons butter
2	onions, chopped
2	bell peppers, chopped
2	cloves garlic, chopped
1½	ribs celery, chopped
1	lb. crab meat, picked over
1	lb. raw shrimp, shelled and deveined and then barely cooked
4	oz. Parmesan cheese
¼	cup Worcestershire sauce
10	drops Tabasco sauce
1⅔	cups cooked rice
	salt and pepper to taste

1. Melt butter. Sauté onions, peppers, garlic, and celery until onion is translucent.
2. Soak eggplant in salt water for 30 minutes. Drain, rinse and steam for 12 minutes or until soft.
3. Combine all ingredients but reserve half of the Parmesan.
4. Taste for seasonings. Put into casserole dish and top with the remaining Parmesan.
5. Bake in a 350°F. oven for 30 minutes or until heated through.

Serves: 6
Preparation: 30 minutes
Cooking: 12 minutes for eggplant, 3 minutes for shrimp, 30 minutes in oven

"You can use all crab meat or all shrimp if you wish. "Sea legs" (imitation crab meat) can be substituted for crab meat. Best when made several hours before serving so that the flavors get a chance to meld. Bring to room temperature before baking. You might want additional Tabasco or Worcestershire in the recipe, but DO NOT use LESS than what is called for."

DRUNKEN FISH CASSEROLE

½	cup butter
1	clove garlic, finely crushed
1	lobster tail, meat chopped
8	medium shrimp, peeled and deveined
8	medium clams in shell, well drained—save liquid
½	cup bourbon
2	cups diced fresh tomatoes
1	cup clam juice
6	oz. red snapper in large dice
6	oz. flounder in large dice
8	oz. fresh scallops
	chopped fresh parsley
	fresh ground pepper to taste
¼	cup butter, melted
	lemon wedges

1. Preheat oven to 350°F.
2. Place large oven-proof sauté pan on stove and heat until hot.
3. Add ½ cup butter and garlic. Quickly rotate pan to coat bottom and sides. Add lobster, shrimp, and clams and toss a couple of minutes.
4. Add bourbon and reduce* liquids.
5. Add tomatoes, clam juice, snapper, flounder, scallops, parsley, pepper. Bring to boil and place in oven for 15 to 20 minutes.
6. Remove from oven. Add ¼ cup butter and squeeze several lemon wedges over all and mix well.
7. Serve garnished with additional lemon wedges.

*See glossary

Serves: 6 to 8
Preparation: 15 to 20 minutes
Cooking: 45 minutes to 1 hour

"A seafood lover's feast in one dish."

MARISCOS CATALANA
(Seafood Catalana)

2	tablespoons diced green pepper
1	tablespoon minced garlic
2	tablespoons diced onion
2	tablespoons olive oil
6	oz. scallops
6	oz. shrimp, shelled and deveined
6	oz. lobster, cut in bite-size pieces
8	oz. clams
4	stone crab claws
2	oz. Spanish brandy (warmed)
1	8-oz. can stewed tomatoes
1	cup beef consommé
	salt to taste

1. Preheat oven to 400°F.
2. Sauté green pepper, garlic and onion in olive oil for 7 minutes.
3. Add washed and prepared seafood. Flambé* with brandy.
4. Add tomatoes, consommé and salt.
5. Bake 12 minutes or until seafood is just done.

*See glossary

Serves: 4
Preparation: 20 minutes
Cooking: 20 minutes

"This is a hearty and delightful seafood stew. Be sure to serve with crusty French bread and a bottle of dry white wine."

CIOPPINO

⅓ cup olive oil
2 cups chopped onions
3 large cloves garlic, chopped
½ cup juice from canned clams
1 1 lb. 12 oz. can stewed tomatoes
   (with celery, green peppers,
   and onions)
1 cup tomato sauce (preferably
   homemade)
1 teaspoon shrimp base
   (available at gourmet speciality
   shops)
½ teaspoon oregano
½ teaspoon basil
¼ teaspoon pepper
            —FISH—
2 lbs. ocean perch
12 pre-cooked shrimp (16-20 per
   lb.)
4 tablespoons titi shrimp (or small
   shrimp), cooked or canned
4 tablespoons chopped clams
8 mussels in shells, steamed just
   until open
1 - 2 lbs. spaghetti

1. Heat oil. Add onions and cook until onions are soft.
2. Add next 8 ingredients. Simmer for 30 minutes.
3. Add perch. Cook until done. Remove perch from sauce and set aside.
4. To serve, place the perch, shrimp, titis, and chopped clams on spaghetti (cooked al dente*). Pour sauce over all.
5. Garnish each plate with two mussels in shell.

*See glossary

Serves: 4
Preparation: 10 minutes
Cooking: 50 to 60 minutes

"A simple variation, this is one of the best you'll ever taste. Be sure to use a great tomato sauce. It's 'bellissimo'!"

CHEF PONZO'S
ZUPPA DI PESCE

2	oysters, shucked
4	littleneck clams
12	mussels
1	lobster, split in half
1	cup olive oil
4	medium squid, cleaned and cut into small rings
4	smelts, finger size
2	fillets of sole (or flounder or turbot), 4 to 8 oz. each
12	sea scallops
12	bay scallops
12	large shrimp
1	cup chablis wine
	few fresh basil leaves
	few capers
	pinch oregano
	white pepper to taste
3	tablespoons granulated garlic powder
	crushed red pepper to taste
3 - 5	cups of your favorite marinara sauce
½ - 1	lb. linguine, cooked al dente*

1. Wash all the shellfish well. Shuck the oysters, saving the liquor.
2. Steam open the clams and mussels. Clean the lobster.
3. In a large frying pan, bring oil to a sizzling point. Put in the split lobster and cover. Turn down the heat and cook for a few minutes, "trembling" the pan so that the lobster

doesn't stick.
4. Remove the cover and add the squid. Very, very delicately, add the clams and mussels in their shells, the shucked oysters, smelts, sole, scallops, and shrimp. Add the wine, the oyster liquor, basil, capers, oregano, pepper, granulated garlic powder, and crushed red pepper.
5. Cover and simmer for 20 minutes. Make sure to "tremble" the pan often so the fish doesn't stick to the bottom. This applies particularly when you are cooking with electric heat which tends to stay hotter than gas. Watch the pan carefully.
6. Add the marinara sauce and finish cooking slowly until the entire sauce becomes thick.
7. Put the linguine in a large serving dish. Starting with the shellfish, arrange all the fish on top of the linguine in an attractive pattern.

*See glossary

Serves: 2 to 4
Preparation: 40 minutes
Cooking: approximately 30 minutes

"Chef Salvatore Ponzo explains that Zuppa di Pesce is a Neopolitan fishermen's dish which gives 'the most intense power to the body and plenty of vitamins and proteins to anyone who likes fish and shellfish.' Legend has it that the dish originated with Neptune, King of the Sea, who was so much in love with a beautiful goddess that he decided to use all of his skill and resources from his watery dominion to create a special dish to please her. The beautiful goddess was so impressed by the meal that she agreed to become his wife."

THE MARDI GRAS
(A fricassee of shrimp and scallops)

2	lbs. medium large shrimp, peeled and deveined
2	lbs. fresh bay scallops
4	oz. butter
1	cup diced red peppers
1	cup diced tomatoes
½	cup minced green onions
1	teaspoon minced garlic
1	teaspoon basil
	salt, pepper, and lemon juice to taste
1	cup vermouth
1	teaspoon beurre manié*
½	cup chopped parsley

1. Sauté shrimp and scallops in butter for 3 minutes over high heat.
2. Add red peppers, tomatoes, green onions, garlic, basil, salt, pepper, lemon juice and vermouth. Cook 3 to 4 minutes.
3. Stir in beurre manié with a whisk.
4. Add chopped parsley and serve immediately.

*See glossary

Serves: 8
Preparation: 30 minutes
Cooking: 8 to 9 minutes

"The flavor is light and mild. For variety you may wish to add oregano or dill."

FETTUCINE
FRUITES DES MER

1	lb. fettucine, cooked al dente*
12	shrimp
	(16 to 20 per lb. size)
1	lb. scallops
3	cloves garlic, minced
⅓	cup olive oil
⅓	cup white wine
⅓	cup fish stock or clam juice
¼	cup lemon juice,
	freshly squeezed
	pinch white pepper
	pinch rosemary
	pinch basil
6	oz. Romano cheese, freshly
	grated

1. Cook fettucine. Put in a warm serving dish; set aside, keeping warm.
2. Heat olive oil in a sauté pan until aroma can be sensed.
3. Add scallops and shrimp and sauté until firm. Remove from pan.
4. Add white wine to pan to deglaze.*
5. Add garlic, lemon juice and stock. Season with white pepper, basil, and rosemary. Stir and cook slightly. Return shrimp and scallops to pan and stir gently.
6. Pour over fettucine and garnish with Romano cheese. Serve immediately.

*See glossary

Serves: 4 to 6
Preparation: 1 hour (includes time cleaning shrimp)
Cooking: 15 minutes

"There's just enough sauce in this dish to enhance the shrimp and scallops without overpowering their wonderfully delicate flavor. Serve as an appetizer or as a main dish."

SEAFOOD LINGUINE

—VELOUTÉ SAUCE—

10	tablespoons butter
8	tablespoons flour
3	tablespoons minced shallots
1	tablespoon minced garlic
1	qt. fish stock*
6	eggs
2½	cups heavy cream
2	tablespoons Dijon mustard
	salt and pepper to taste

1. Sauté shallots and garlic in 2 tablespoons of butter until golden. Set aside.
2. Melt 8 tablespoons of butter and stir in the flour. Cook until slightly brown.
3. Stir in fish stock, little by little, and continue to stir until thickened.
4. Add reserved garlic and shallots.
5. Quickly whisk the eggs into the heavy cream and then whisk into the thickened sauce.
6. Add mustard, salt and pepper to taste.

—SEAFOOD—

10	tablespoons butter
4	4-oz. lobster tails cleaned and shelled
12	large shrimp, peeled and deveined
2	cups diced clams (fresh or canned), rinsed and drained if canned

16	medium asparagus spears, fresh or frozen
2	tablespoons brandy
½	cup freshly grated Parmesan cheese
1	lb. linguine, cooked al dente*

1. Melt 6 tablespoons of butter in a heavy pan.
2. Add lobster and shrimp and cook over a low heat for 2 to 3 minutes.
3. Add diced clams and cook for 2 more minutes.
4. Pour brandy over seafood and flambé.*
5. Toss linguine with 4 tablespoons melted butter and salt and pepper.
6. Pour Velouté Sauce over the noodles, toss and simmer for 5 minutes.
7. Steam asparagus until tender.
8. To serve: Divide noodles equally onto 4 plates and top each portion with seafood, asparagus, and sauce. Pass Parmesan separately.

*See glossary

Serves: 4
Preparation: 30 minutes
Cooking: approximately 30 minutes

"A rich but delicate sauce complements the shellfish."

BAKED CRAB
AND
SHRIMP SUPREME

3	6½-oz. cans lump crab meat, picked over
1½	lbs. boiled shrimp (small or medium)
3	green peppers, chopped
3	onions, chopped
1½	cups chopped celery
4	cups mayonnaise
3	cups buttered bread crumbs
3	teaspoons Worcestershire sauce
	salt and pepper to taste

1. Preheat oven to 350°F.
2. Combine all ingredients except bread crumbs.
3. Put in a baking dish and top with crumbs.
4. Bake for 30 minutes.

Serves: 6 to 8
Preparation: 10 minutes
Cooking: 30 minutes

"The Driftwood serves this in small casserole dishes for luncheon. It's quite easy to do."

SHRIMPS
AND SCALLOPS
AU PERNOD

2	tablespoons butter
1	bunch leeks, finely chopped (white part only)
1½	lbs. large shrimp, peeled, deveined and halved
1½	lbs. large sea scallops
½	cup heavy cream
2	oz. Pernod or Anisette
2	cups cooked rice
	salt and pepper

1. Melt butter. Add leeks, shrimp, and scallops and sauté for 2 minutes.
2. Add cream, Anisette, salt and pepper. Cook for another 5 minutes or until the shrimp are done and the sauce is thick.
3. Serve over hot rice with a fresh vegetable or two on the side.

Serves: 4 to 6
Preparation: 20 minutes
Cooking: 7 minutes

"If leek is not available substitute 6 shallots finely diced or a generous ½ cup of diced sweet onion. You might try this over spinach."

PAELLA VALENCIANA

½	cup olive oil
1	onion, chopped
1	green pepper, chopped
½	cup whole tomatoes
3	garlic cloves, minced
1	bay leaf
½	lb. pork, cut in chunks
½	frying chicken, cut in 4 pieces
1	lb. lobster, cleaned and cut in chunks
½	lb. shrimp, cleaned and peeled
8	oysters, shucked
8	scallops, washed and drained
8	mussels in shells, scrubbed and debearded
4	clams in shells, scrubbed
4	stone crab claws, cleaned and drained
1	lb. red snapper, cut in chunks
6	cups fresh seafood or chicken stock (or bottled clam juice)
1½	cups rice
1	teaspoon salt
	pinch saffron
¼	cup white wine
	small green peas, asparagus and sliced pimientos for garnish

1. Preheat oven to 350°F.
2. Heat oil in a heavy casserole. Add onions and green pepper and fry until limp but not brown.
3. Chop tomatoes in blender. Add tomatoes, garlic and bay leaf to casserole and cook for 5 minutes.
4. Add pork and chicken and sauté until tender, stirring to prevent sticking or burning.
5. Add seafood and stock. Bring to a boil and add rice, salt, and saffron and stir.
6. Bring to a boil again, cover, and bake in the oven for 20 minutes.
7. Cook the peas and asparagus.
8. When ready to serve, sprinkle wine over the paella. Garnish with the peas, asparagus, and pimiento.

Serves: 4 to 8
Preparation: 45 minutes
Cooking: 35 to 40 minutes

"This extremely versatile dish allows you to use almost any native seafood in lieu of the above ingredients. It is the national dish of Spain. Our hats off to the Gonsmart family."

SHRIMP JAMBALAYA

1	medium green pepper
1	small Spanish onion
2	celery ribs
6	oz. smoked ham
3	large cloves garlic, minced
⅛	cup olive oil
12	large shrimp, peeled and deveined
	dash of curry
3	tablespoons Worcestershire sauce
1	16-oz. can whole peeled tomatoes
½	cup cooked rice
	salt and pepper to taste

1. Cut pepper, onion, celery, and smoked ham into thin strips.
2. Sauté garlic in oil until golden brown.
3. Add vegetables and ham. Cook for 5 minutes over medium heat.
4. Add raw shrimp, curry, Worcestershire and tomatoes.
5. Cook for about 10 minutes, or until shrimp are almost done.
6. Add rice, salt and pepper to taste and cook for 2 minutes longer.

Serves: 2 to 4
Preparation: 20 minutes
Cooking: 20 minutes

"This is one of the best jambalayas we've tasted. Vinton's has been widely acclaimed for this easy but excellent recipe."

Notes

EMMERT

SOUPS AND CHOWDERS

SHELL FISH CHOWDER

1	oz. crab meat, cut in chunks
3	medium shrimp, peeled and deveined
2	mussels, well scrubbed
1	oz. chopped clams
¼	lb. bacon
½	cup finely chopped onions
2	cloves garlic, minced
¼	lb. butter
2	cups Gorton's New England clam chowder
2	cups heavy cream
1	teaspoon Minor's shrimp base (optional)

1. Steam open the shellfish.
2. Cook the bacon to the chewy, not crisp, stage. Drain and dice.
3. Melt butter and sauté onions and garlic until golden.
4. Stir in canned clam chowder, cream, and shrimp base. Cook until blended and hot. Pour over the steamed shellfish and serve with crackers.

Serves: 4
Preparation: 5 minutes
Cooking: 10 minutes

"Serve this in a deep bowl making sure that everyone gets some fish. This should be served piping hot."

FLORIDA
FISH CHOWDER

1	quart fish* or chicken stock
2	cups finely chopped conch and/ or fish
1	cup finely chopped green pepper
1	cup finely chopped celery
1	cup finely chopped onion
¾-1	cup instant potato flour
1	cup milk
1	cup heavy cream
	salt, pepper, Tabasco sauce to taste

1. Sauté all vegetables and conch/fish without browning them.
2. Add sautéed vegetables to the heated stock and cook over medium heat approximately 10 minutes.
3. Add the instant potato flour, then the milk and the cream. Simmer.

*See glossary

Serves: 6 to 8
Preparation: 15 minutes
Cooking: 30 minutes

"Make this with a variety of fish."

BAHAMIAN CONCH CHOWDER

(40 to 50 or more bowls, not cups. This is a double batch.)

1	lb. salt pork, chopped
2	lbs. butter or margarine
4	lbs. onions, chopped
4	cups plain flour
4	46-oz. cans clam juice (American clam juice brand if possible)
6	qts. fresh clam juice
2	large cans tomato juice
2	No. 10 cans Libby crushed tomatoes
2	stalks celery, chopped
6	lbs. chopped carrots, cooked
12	lbs. diced potatoes, cooked
½	cup Accent
2	tablespoons white pepper
2	tablespoons cayenne red ground pepper
1	fifth sherry wine
8	lbs. diced Bahamian conch (tenderize and cook in pressure cooker 30 minutes)

1. Melt the butter in a *very large* pan and sauté the onions until golden over medium heat.
2. Stir in the flour and cook until slightly brown.
3. Add the clam juice and tomato juice, a little at a time, stirring constantly.
4. Add the rest of the ingredients and mix.
5. Simmer until the vegetables are tender.

Serves: a very large crowd
Preparation: 1 hour
Cooking: 30 to 60 minutes

"Chef Steve Knight says it tastes even better the second day it's heated."

NEW ENGLAND CLAM CHOWDER

¼	cup margarine, melted
2	cups coarsely chopped celery
2	cloves garlic, crushed
5	cups coarsely chopped Spanish onion
4	bay leaves
¼	cup margarine
¼	cup flour
3	tablespoons clam stock* mixed with 1¾ cups water
1	lb. clams, fresh (steamed), frozen (defrosted and sautéed in a little butter) or canned (rinsed and drained)
1	tablespoon thyme
1	teaspoon salt
1	cup potatoes, peeled, cooked and diced
10	oz. heavy cream

1. Sauté celery, onion, garlic, and bay leaves in margarine until vegetables are tender. Set aside.
2. Melt other ¼ cup of margarine. Stir in flour to make a roux and stir until it starts to brown. Gradually whisk in clam-water mixture. Stir rapidly until smooth and then simmer for 10 minutes or so, stirring occasionally.
3. Add sautéed vegetables, thyme, and salt to the clam mixture and simmer for 5 minutes.
4. Add clams and potatoes. Gradually add the cream and stir continuously until warm and well mixed.

*See glossary

Serves: 4
Preparation: 20 minutes
Cooking: 30 minutes

"Transplanted New Englanders (and everybody else) will like this creamy chowder. Enjoy at home or at Bentley's amid the beautiful surroundings."

241

CONCH CHOWDER

(Made from an old Minorcan family recipe)

⅛	lb. salt pork, chopped fine
2	onions, chopped fine
1	bell pepper, chopped fine
1-2	datil* peppers (or hottest pepper for substitute)
12	oz. conch meat or clams (well cleaned)
3	cups canned tomatoes, chopped
2	cups canned potatoes, diced
½	cup tomato puree
½	tablespoon thyme
½	tablespoon salt
½	tablespoon fresh ground pepper
1-2	bay leaves, crushed

1. Sauté pork in large pot. Remove and set aside.
2. Add onions, bell peppers and sauté. Add hot peppers.
3. Add reserved pork and remaining ingredients.
4. Bring to boil 15 minutes. Simmer 45 minutes to 1 hour.

*Datil peppers are very hot and may be difficult to find. The Ponce family has them "custom" grown for their seafood dishes. If you can't find your own datil peppers write David Ponce and he'll send you the name of a supplier.

Serves: 6 to 8
Preparation: 15 minutes
Cooking: 1 hour

"Purchase conch at your seafood market and try this exciting chowder!"

OYSTER STEW

4	cups light cream
3	dozen fresh shucked oysters—save oyster liquor
½	cup dry white wine
2	tablespoons butter
	salt, white pepper, and cayenne to taste
	fresh parsley

1. Poach the oysters in their own liquor and wine until their edges curl and they plump up.
2. Place in a double boiler. Add cream, salt, pepper, and cayenne. Heat until very hot.
3. Add butter and parsley.

Serves: 6
Preparation: 30 minutes—includes shucking
Cooking: 15 minutes

"This can be held for several hours without curdling. This is a simple recipe with mouth-watering taste. Serve with cheddar cheese sticks and oyster crackers, or have it at Derby Lane just before the dog races!"

243

CHEF WATSON'S CONCH CHOWDER

2	conch, cleaned
1	large onion, diced
3	celery stalks, diced
1	large potato, peeled and diced
1	small onion, diced
2	strips bacon, diced
1	green pepper, diced
1	carrot, peeled and diced
	Tabasco sauce to taste
	pinch of thyme
	pinch of basil
3	bay leaves
	salt and pepper
1	small tomato, diced

1. Cover the conch with water and simmer until the conch is tender. The amount of time varies with the size of the conch.
2. Remove the conch from the water and dice. Save the water.
3. Sauté all of the vegetables (except the potato and tomato) in a pan along with the bacon until they are crisp-tender.
4. Put vegetables, bacon, potato, seasoning and conch in a pot along with the water which you have saved and strained. Simmer until vegetables are tender. Add tomato and cook for 5 more minutes. Correct seasonings.

Serves: 4 to 6
Preparation: 20 minutes (plus conch cooking time)
Cooking: approximately 30 minutes

"The conch for this recipe is tenderized by cooking, not by pounding. You probably will have most of the ingredients on hand, so it is a great recipe to make if you stumble upon some conch on the beach."

LA BISQUE DE NEPTUNE AU SHERRY
(Seafood Bisque)

—LOBSTER ESSENCE—

3	New Zealand lobster tail shells
1½	oz. cognac
½	onion
½	large tomato
½	celery stalk
½	carrot
½	tablespoon soybean oil
	salt, whole black pepper
	bay leaves
8	oz. fish fumé*

1. Shell the lobster tails and set meat aside.
2. Dice all vegetables to ½ inch.
3. Sauté the onions in the hot oil in a large pan.
4. Add the lobster shells, flip them over until they become red.
5. Add the carrot, celery, and tomato. Cook for 1 minute.
6. Add the cognac and flambé*.
7. Add the spices and fish fumé.
8. Bring to boil, remove from heat, and let cool.
9. Strain before serving.

—LOBSTER—

3	New Zealand lobster tails, meat only
6	oz. baby shrimp
5	oz. snow crab meat
5	oz. California white wine
½	oz. cognac
1	oz. sherry
½	pint heavy cream
8	oz. lobster essence
8	oz. fish fumé*
1½	oz. soybean oil
½	oz. shallots
1½	oz. butter
2	oz. flour

1. Cut the reserved lobster meat into medallions (4 per tail).
2. In a hot pot, sauté the shallots. Add the lobster and shrimp. Cook slightly.
3. Deglaze* with the cognac.
4. Add the flour and mix until a thick paste appears.
5. Add the white wine, the fish fumé, and the lobster essence.
6. Simmer for 15 minutes, then add the crab meat.
7. Turn off the heat, add the cream and sherry, and serve.

*See glossary

Serves: 6
Preparation: 30 minutes
Cooking: 30 minutes

"A real "Lucullan" feast!"

SPINACH AND CLAM SOUP

½	medium onion, diced
4	strips of bacon, diced
4	anchovy fillets, minced
1	clove garlic, minced
1	stick butter
2	tablespoons flour
4	cups chicken stock or broth
1	10½-oz. package spinach, thawed and squeezed dry
2	6½-oz. cans clams, rinsed and drained
1	cup heavy cream
	salt and pepper
	Pernod (optional)

1. Heat a heavy skillet over medium-high heat. Add onion, bacon, anchovies, and garlic and sauté lightly. Remove from heat and set aside.
2. Melt the butter in a large saucepan over medium heat. Add flour and stir constantly for 2 to 3 minutes.
3. Slowly whisk in stock and bring to a boil.
4. Add reserved mixture, spinach, and clams. Bring back to the boil, stirring occasionally.
5. Add cream and bring to a boil again. Add salt and pepper to taste and a dash of Pernod if desired.

Serves: 6 to 8
Preparation: 10 minutes (plus thawing time for spinach)
Cooking: 10 to 15 minutes

"This is a fresh-tasting soup that is good to serve at any time of the year. If you wish to substitute fresh clams for canned, steam them open, drain, and chop."

COLD AVOCADO CRAB SOUP

2	avocados, peeled
1	4-oz. can crab meat
¼	cup minced celery
½	cup sour cream
1	cup heavy cream
	salt and white pepper to taste
	dash Tabasco sauce
	toasted almonds

1. Dice one avocado in ¼" cubes. Puree the other one in a blender or food processor.
2. Combine crab meat (picked over and drained), celery, sour cream, heavy cream, salt and pepper, Tabasco and the avocados.
3. Mix thoroughly and chill for several hours.
4. If the consistency is too thick, before serving thin with heavy cream.
5. Garnish with toasted almonds.

Serves: 4 to 5
Preparation: 20 minutes (plus time for chilling)
Cooking: 5 minutes

"Make sure that you make this far enough in advance so that it is very well chilled."

EMMERT

SAUCED
LOBSTER

DILL SAUCE

1 cup watercress leaves
¼ cup minced scallions
2 tablespoons minced parsley
1 cup mayonnaise
3 anchovy fillets, chopped
3 tablespoons lemon juice
 to taste
 salt and pepper to taste
3-4 tablespoons minced fresh dill
½ cup sour cream

1. Put all ingredients (except the dill and sour cream) into a blender or food processor. Blend until smooth.
2. Add the dill and blend 1 or 2 seconds, until the dill has just been absorbed.
3. Remove from blender or processor and whisk in sour cream. Add salt and pepper to taste if necessary.
4. Chill thoroughly before serving.

Yield: about 1½ cups of sauce
Preparation: 10 minutes
Chilling time: 1 hour or more

"Dill sauce is good on poached or broiled fish and shellfish. Marina Polvay, Executive Chef, has once again outdone herself!"

SEAFOOD SAUCE
(For crêpes or fish)

¼   cup butter
1   small onion, diced
1   cup sliced mushrooms
    roux* (3 tablespoons butter
    and 3 tablespoons flour)
1½ cups milk
4   tablespoons sherry
1   teaspoon Worcestershire sauce
1   dash Tabasco sauce
    salt and pepper
½   lb. crab meat, picked over
½   lb. fish fillets, such as sole, cut in
    pieces (include only if used to
    stuff crêpes)
½   lb. scallops, cut in small pieces
½   lb. shrimp, peeled, deveined and
    cut in small pieces
2   tablespoons chopped parsley

1. Melt the butter and sauté onions and mushrooms until onions are golden. Set aside.
2. Make a roux and gradually add the milk and then the sherry.
3. Stir constantly until it starts to thicken. Add seafood and spices and cook until seafood is done. Add mushrooms and onions.
4. Sprinkle with parsley.

*See glossary

Serves: 8 if fish sauce, 6 for crêpe stuffing
Preparation: 10 minutes
Cooking: approximately 15 minutes

"If using to stuff crêpes, make the sauce at the last minute. Brush filled, rolled crêpes with a little melted butter and put under broiler for a minute or two. Would be scrumptious over rice or chopped spinach."

FENNEL SAUCE

	roux* (3 T. butter and 3 T. flour)
1	qt. fish stock*
1	small bunch of fresh fennel
1	tablespoon butter
2	shallots, chopped
¼	cup white wine
½	cup heavy cream
2	egg yolks
	salt and white pepper to taste

1. Add stock to roux to thicken slightly.
2. Steam the leafy green part of the fennel 2 minutes and add to stock.
3. Simmer 20 minutes
4. In a separate pan, sauté shallots in butter, add wine and reduce.*
5. Add warmed cream to wine mixture and reduce again.
6. Add this mixture to stock and fennel.
7. Puree and strain.
8. Add egg yolks, one at a time, stirring constantly. Do not boil after adding yolks.
9. Correct for seasonings.
10. Braise bulb of fennel cut in quarters as you would celery or endive. Use lemon juice to keep it white. Use for garnish.

*See glossary

Yield: 1 quart
Preparation: 20 minutes
Cooking: 30 minutes

"Cafe Chauveron suggests using this sauce with fresh poached salmon. Or you might try it on baked or broiled snapper, grouper, or stuffed trout."

SHRIMP SAUCE

1   cup mayonnaise
¾   cup catsup
1   oz. Worcestershire sauce
1   oz. horseradish
½   oz. A.B. hot sauce

1. Mix thoroughly and serve.

Preparation: 5 minutes
Yields: 2 cups

"This is light in color because of the mayonnaise, but don't be deceived—it's VERY tangy!"

MUSTARD SAUCE

4   oz. Coleman's English mustard
1   qt. mayonnaise
½   cup A-1 sauce
½   cup Lea & Perrins Worcestershire sauce
4   oz. cream

1. In a bowl, combine the mustard, mayonnaise, A-1 sauce and Worcestershire sauce, using a wire whisk. Beat until smooth.
2. Slowly add the cream and continue to beat until you reach proper sauce consistency. Sauce can be refrigerated for future.

Serves: A crowd!
Preparation: 5 minutes
Yields: 5 cups

"This is the famous sauce for stone crabs, but it can also be used on beef."

SHRIMP SAUCE IN TARRAGON CREAM

2	tablespoons butter
2	tablespoons flour
1	cup heavy cream
½	cup clam juice (bottled)
1	cup white wine
½	lb. cooked shrimp, shelled, deveined and split
2	teaspoons chopped parsley
½	teaspoon tarragon

1. Melt butter in heavy pan and stir in flour. Stir over a low heat for 5 minutes.
2. Remove from heat and whisk in cream, clam juice, and wine.
3. Return to heat and stir constantly until sauce thickens.
4. Stir in shrimp, parsley, and tarragon until shrimp are just heated through.
5. Serve over Shrimp Mousse*

*See index

Serves: 6
Preparation: 5 minutes
Cooking: 10 to 15 minutes

"This is a delicious sauce! Double the recipe and serve over rice. If fresh tarragon is not available, use dried, but do not leave it out."

LOBSTER
SAUCE CHAUVERON

1	1-lb. lobster, cleaned
2	carrots, chopped
1	onion, chopped
1	leek, chopped
3	shallots, chopped
2	celery stalks, chopped
1	head (bulb) of garlic, chopped
2	thyme leaves
1	bay leaf
1	cup tomato puree
	pinch of tarragon
	dash cognac, white wine, salt, cayenne pepper
1	qt. fish stock*
	beurre manié* (6 oz. butter, 6 oz. flour)
1	qt. heavy cream

1. Cut tail off lobster and split in half. Chop the head and body in as small pieces as possible. Crack the claws.
2. Sauté the lobster in hot oil in a large saucepan until very red in color.
3. Add the chopped vegetables and sauté for 10 to 15 minutes.
4. Deglaze* with white wine and cognac. Cook for 2 minutes.
5. Add fish stock, tomato puree, and the rest of the seasonings. Bring to a boil and cook 15 minutes.
6. Take out claws and tail and remove meat. Reserve meat.
7. With a slotted spoon, remove the vegetables and the lobster shells from the sauce. Bring the sauce to a boil and add the beurre manié, stirring until the sauce thickens. Strain the sauce.
8. In a separate pan, bring 1 quart of heavy cream to a boil. Add the above lobster sauce to the cream and stir.
9. Chop up the reserved lobster meat and fold into the sauce. Adjust the seasonings.

Serves: 8
Preparation: 1 hour
Cooking: 45 to 60 minutes

*See glossary

"This extravaganza lends itself to napping a mousse beautifully."

ORANGE
MUSTARD SAUCE

¾ cup orange marmalade
¼ cup chicken or beef stock
2 tablespoons fresh lemon juice
1 teaspoon dry mustard
few drops hot pepper sauce

1. Combine all ingredients. Enjoy with Shrimp Almendrina*
or fried shrimp.

*See index

Yields: about 1 cup

"You'll love this distinct flavor, 'Ole'."

CURRY SAUCE
Á LA MONIQUE

1	cup mayonnaise
1	cup sour cream
1	clove garlic, minced
2	teaspoons curry powder
3	tablespoons olive oil
3	tablespoons sugar
	juice from 2 medium oranges
2	tablespoons fresh lemon juice
2	tablespoons chopped
	mango chutney
	salt and freshly ground pepper
1	oz. Bombay gin

1. Combine mayonnaise and sour cream in medium mixing bowl and set aside.
2. In small saucepan or skillet over low heat, sauté garlic and curry powder in olive oil until well blended.
3. Remove from heat and stir into mayonnaise-sour cream mixture.
4. Add sugar, orange and lemon juices, chutney, salt and pepper to taste and blend until smooth. Chill.
5. Just before serving, stir gin into sauce.

Serves: 8
Preparation: 15 minutes (plus time for chilling)
Cooking: 5 minutes

"This curry sauce will add the final touch to cooked shell or fin fish."

SIMPLE
TARTARE SAUCE

1	tablespoon chopped onions
1	cup mayonnaise
1	tablespoon dill pickle, chopped
½	teaspoon granulated garlic

1. Mix ingredients well. Chill.

Yields: 1 cup
Preparation: 5 minutes

"Here's a good old standby... thin with vinegar if too thick."

COCKTAIL SAUCE

1   cup catsup (may substitute chili
     sauce)
1   tablespoon horseradish
1   teaspoon Luziana hot sauce
½   teaspoon lemon juice

1. Mix ingredients well. Chill.

Yields: 1 cup
Preparation: 5 minutes

"Decrease hot sauce if necessary—this has a nice zing! A good basic cocktail sauce."

TEMPURA SAUCE
(TEN-TSUYU)
(Light dipping sauce)

¼ cup chicken stock (may substitute broth)
2 teaspoons mirin (sweet sake)
¼ cup shoyu (soy sauce)
½ teaspoon fresh ginger, peeled and chopped fine
white radish, grated

1. Add mirin, shoyu and ginger to chicken stock.
2. Garnish with grated white radish. Serve in small bowl for dipping.

Yields: ½ cup
Preparation: 5 minutes

"Easy to make, great dipping."

MUSTARD
FRUIT SAUCE

1   cup mustard fruits chopped
     (available in gourmet specialty
     shops)
1   cup apricot preserves
2   teaspoons Grey Poupon mustard

1. Blend all ingredients in blender or food processor into a
   coarse sauce (do not puree or liquify).
2. Chill. Serve cold or at room temperature.

Yields: 2 cups
Preparation: 2 minutes (plus time for chilling)

"This would be delicious with fried shrimp."

Notes

Glossary Of Terms

Al dente
Literally means "to the tooth" in Italian. The food, particularly pasta, is just barely cooked.

Bechamel Sauce
A basic sauce that serves as a base for many classic sauces. To use for fish recipes:
1. Make a roux with 1 tablespoon each of butter and flour. Cook for 2 minutes.
2. Gradually whisk in ¾ cup milk and ¼ cup fish stock (or all milk). Whisk until smooth.
3. Cook over low heat until milk is warmed through. Taste for seasoning. Makes about 1 cup.

Beurre Manié
Mix 1 teaspoon each of flour and butter (or equal amounts of both). Rub with the heel of your hand until blended and form into a ball(s). Can be frozen.

Blanch
Plunge food into boiling water for 30 to 60 seconds, then put under cold running water to stop the cooking process.

Brown Sauce (Quick)
1. Melt 2 tablespoons butter.
2. Stir in ½ clove of garlic and remove after 10 seconds.
3. Stir in 2 tablespoons flour to make a roux.
4. Cook 2 minutes.
5. Whisk in 1 cup canned beef bouillon or broth.
6. Continue whisking until broth comes to a boil.
7. Season to taste.

Butterfly
Cut against the grain or cut lengthwise, leaving flesh attached. This is done for appearance and to tenderize.

Chop
Separate into small pieces—the sharper the knife the easier it is to do.

Clam Stock
Strain liquid remaining after steaming clams open. Bottled clam juice can be used instead but reduce the amount of salt called for in recipe.

Clarified Butter
1. Slowly heat butter until completely melted.
2. Carefully skim off the whey (white matter) that rises to the top. The remaining clear (clarified) butter keeps for at least a week if tightly covered and refrigerated.

Court Bouillon
trimmings (bones, head, tail, etc.) from fish
1 onion stuck with cloves
1 carrot, 1 celery stalk - cut in thirds
4-5 sprigs parsley
2 cups water
1 cup white wine

1. Simmer for 20 minutes.
2. Strain and taste for seasonings.

If using for shellfish recipe, replace fish trimmings with appropriate shells from lobster, crab, etc. In a pinch, use bottled clam juice.

De-glaze
Use a liquid (water, broth, or wine) to "clean" a pan. Turn heat under pan to high - add required liquid and use a wooden spoon to scrape up particles.

Dice
Cut into small cubes, usually less than ½" square.

Fish Stock
See court bouillon.

Fish Velouté Sauce
Use fish stock as part of the liquid when making bechamel sauce.

Flambé (flame)
Cover food lightly with spirits and carefully ignite. It is to add flavor or beauty when serving.

Garlic Butter

Mash 4 to 6 cloves garlic and mince. Work into 1 stick softened butter. Refrigerate and use as needed.

Hollandaise Sauce (Blender)

3 egg yolks
2 teaspoons lemon juice
¼ teaspoon salt
dash of cayenne
½ cup butter, melted

1. In blender or food processor, beat yolks until thickened. Beat in juice, salt, and cayenne.
2. Pour hot butter in a stream with machine running. Serve in warmed bowl.

Yield: 1 cup

Hollandaise Sauce (Classic)

¾ cup butter, melted
3 egg yolks, beaten
4 teaspoons lemon juice
dash of salt and cayenne

1. In top of double boiler, add ⅓ of the butter. Beat in eggs and juice with wire whisk.
2. Add remaining butter slowly, beating constantly until mixture thickens - never allowing water to boil.
3. Stir in seasonings and serve.

Yield: ¾ cup

Julienne

Cut into thin strips or matchlike sticks.

Mince

Chop into very tiny pieces.

Poach

Cook food gently in liquid that is barely simmering.

Reduce

Boil down liquid until it is less; to concentrate flavor.

Roux

Used as a base for many sauces.
Melt butter and stir in flour (recipes usually call for equal amounts of both). Cook, stirring constantly for several minutes until golden or brown as recipe indicates.

Sweat

Let drops of moisture form on the surface of food. Usually done in pan over low heat with buttered wax paper covering food and topped with the pan lid. This helps to intensify flavor.

Veal Stock (Sauce)

4 veal bones, rinsed and cracked
1 carrot, peeled and chopped
1 onion, chopped
3 stalks celery, chopped
several parsley sprigs
1 bay leaf
6 whole cloves, slightly bruised
¼ teaspoon thyme

1. Simmer for several hours.
2. Strain, taste for seasoning and cool.

Vin Rouge

Add red wine to fish velouté sauce.

Zest

The peel (not the white pith) part of citrus fruit often poached, candied or finely chopped - used as a flavor enhancer or for garnish.

"Underwater" Ingredients Were Purchased At The Following Stores In Florida:

Ward's Seafood Markets
St. Petersburg and Clearwater

Publix Supermarkets

Albertson's

Winn Dixie

Many thanks for your cooperation and service!

Additional Thanks To:

Gulf and South Atlantic Fisheries Development Foundation, Inc.

Florida Restaurant Association

The Florida Chamber of Commerce

Food Editors and Food Writers in Florida

bj Altschul

Hard-To-Find Ingredients May Be Purchased By Mail Order Through The Following Source:

The Market Place
Fancy Food Buying Office
22 East Flagler Street
Miami, Florida 33101

Notes

Many thanks to these restaurants who have contributed their favorite recipes:

Andrew's 2nd Act
Tallahassee
Bagatelle
Key West
Bentley's
Clearwater
Bernard's
Boynton Beach
Bimini Sea Shack
Fort Lauderdale
Bob Heilman's Beachcomber
Clearwater Beach
Bon Appétit
Dunedin
Brothers, Too
Tampa
Buttonwood Bar B-Q
Sanibel Island
Cafe Chauveron
Bay Harbor Island
Cap's Seafood Restaurant
St. Augustine
Captain Jim's Conch Hut
St. Augustine
The Captain's Table
Deerfield Beach
Casa Vecchia
Fort Lauderdale
The Catfish Place
St. Cloud

Chadwick's
Captiva Island
Chalet Suzanne
Lake Wales
Chateau Parisien
Tampa
Chez Emile
Key West
Coffee Cup
Pensacola
The Colony Restaurant
Longboat Key
The Columbia Restaurant
Tampa
Sarasota
St. Augustine
The Conch
Islamorada
Crabpot Restaurant and Lounge
Fort Lauderdale
Crab Pot
Deerfield Beach
The Crab Trap
Palmetto
Cruise Inn
Palmetto
Derby Lane Restaurant
St. Petersburg
The Dining Galleries
at the Fountainebleau Hilton
Miami Beach
Dominique's
Miami Beach
Washington, D.C.
The Driftwood Restaurant
Pensacola

El Bodegon Castilla
Miami
**Empress Lilly Riverboat
at Walt Disney World Village**
Lake Buena Vista
**Fisherman's Deck
at Walt Disney World Village**
Lake Buena Vista
The Forge
Miami Beach
Frogs Landing
Cedar Key
Gary's Duck Inn
Orlando
Gator Grill
Marco Island
**Half Shell Raw Bar
at Lands End Village**
Key West
Joe's Stone Crab Restaurant
Miami Beach
Julia Mae's
Carrabelle
**King Charles Restaurant
at the Don Cesar Hotel**
St. Petersburg Beach
Klaus' Cuisine
Holly Hill
Kyushu Restaurant—Sushi Bar
Key West
La Reserve
Fort Lauderdale
**La Terraza De Marti
(La Te Da)**
Key West

Lauro's Ristorante
Tampa
Le Petite Fleur
Tampa
The Lincoln Restaurant
Tampa
The Lobster Pot
Redington Shores
Louis Pappas Riverside Restaurant
Tarpon Springs
Mai-Kai
Fort Lauderdale
Maison & Jardin Restaurant
Altamonte Springs
Marker 88
Islamorada
Marty's Steaks
Tampa
New River Storehouse
Fort Lauderdale
O'Steen's
St. Augustine
Park Plaza Gardens
Winter Park
Pate's
Naples
Pepin's
St. Petersburg
Peter's Place
St. Petersburg
Petite Marmite
Palm Beach
Pier House
Key West

The Plum Room
Fort Lauderdale
Raimondo's
Coral Gables
Raintree Restaurant
St. Augustine
The Red Snapper
Daytona Beach Shores
Ristorante Mama Mia
Tampa
Rollande et Pierre
St. Petersburg
Sea Grill
Fort Lauderdale
The Seaport Chef
St. Petersburg
The Seaport Inn
New Port Richey
Selena's
Tampa
Silas Dent's Restaurant and Oyster Bar
St. Petersburg Beach
Siple's Garden Seat
Clearwater
The Sovereign Restaurant
Gainesville
Swanson's Wine Bar●Bistro
Clearwater
Ted Peters Smoked Fish
St. Petersburg
The Vilano Seafood Shack
St. Augustine
Villa Nova
Winter Park
Vinton's
Coral Gables

Vinton's New Orleans
Lake Wales
Westwind'r-Sushi Bar
Hyatt Regency
Tampa
The Wine Cellar
North Redington Beach
The Wine Cellar Restaurant
Fort Lauderdale
The Yearling Restaurant
Cross Creek

References

Alberson, Sarah D. (1968). *The Blue Sea Cookbook.* New York: Hastings House.

Artman, L.P. Jr. (1975). *Conch Cooking.* Key West: Florida Keys Printing and Publishing.

Beard, James (1976). *James Beard's New Fish Cookery.* Boston: Little, Brown and Co.

Carrier, Robert (1965). *The Connoisseurs' Cookbook.* New York: Random House.

Claiborne, Craig (1975). *Craig Claiborne's Favorites from The New York Times.* New York, N.Y.: Quadrangle. The New York Times Book Co.

Cofield, Tom (1976). *The Fisherman's Guide to North America.* New York: Grosset and Dunlop.

Collins, Rima and Richard (1976). *The Pleasures of Seafood.* New York: Holt, Rhinehart and Winston.

Davidson, Alan (1979). *North Atlantic Seafood.* New York: The Viking Press.

Davis, Frank (1983). *Frank Davis Seafood Notebook.* Gretna, La.: Pelican Publishing Co.

Davis, J. Charles 2nd (1967). *Fish Cookery.* South Brunswick and New York: Barnes & Co., Inc.

Day, Bunny (1961). *Catch 'em and Cook 'em.* Garden City, N.Y.: Doubleday & Co.

Day, Bunny. *Hook 'em and Cook 'em.* New York : Gramercy Publishing Company.

Detrick, Mia. *Sushi.* San Francisco: Chronicle Books.

Fisher, M.F.K. (1941). *Consider the Oyster.* New York: Duell, Sloan and Pearce.

Florida Cooperative Extension Service, G022 McCarty Hall, University of Florida, Gainesville, FL 32611.

Florida Department of Natural Resources—Bureau of Marketing and Extension Services, Tallahassee, FL 32303.

Gibbons, Euell (1964). *Stalking the Blue-Eyed Scallop.* New York: David McKay Co., Inc.

The Good Cook Technique/Recipes—Shellfish. Alexandria: Time-Life Books.

(1980) *Guide to Japanese Food and Restaurants.* Los Angeles, Calif.: Pacific Friend Int'l.

Gulf and South Atlantic Fisheries Development Foundation, Inc.: Tampa, FL 33609

Hawkins, Arthur (1970). *The Complete Seafood Cookbook.* Englewood Cliffs: Prentice-Hall Inc.

Headstrom, Richard (1979). *Lobsters, Crabs, Shrimp and Their Relatives.* S. Brunswick, N.Y.: A.S. Barnes and Co.

London, Sheryl and Mel (1980). *The Fish Lovers' Cookbook.* Emmaus, Pa.: The Rodale Press.

McClane, A.J. (1978). *McClane's Field Guide to Saltwater Fishes.* New York: Holt, Rhinehart and Winston.

Marine Advisory Program, Florida Cooperative Extension Service, University of Florida, Gainesville, FL 32611.

Maryland Department of Economic and Community Development, Office of Seafood Marketing. (1982). *Maryland Seafood Cookbook III.* Annapolis, Maryland.

Morris, Dan and Moore, Matilda (1966). *Savor of the Sea.* New York: Macmillan Co.

Morris, Dan and Inez (1972). *The Complete Fish Cookbook.* Indianapolis and New York: Bobbs-Merrill Co.

Multi-County Extension Bureau, Largo, FL.

Omae, Kinjiro and Tachibana, Yuzuru (1981). *The Book of Sushi:* Tokyo, New York & San Francisco; Kodansha International Ltd.

Raymond, Dorothy (1981). *Catch and Cook Seafood.* St. Petersburg: The Great Outdoors Publishing Co.

Romagnoli, Margaret and G. Franco (1975). *The Romagnolis' Table.* Boston: Atlantic Monthly Press (Division of Little Brown & Co.).

Rombauer, Irma and Becker, Marion R. (1964). *The Joy of Cooking.* New York: New American Library.

Schulz, Eva Jean. (1966). *Shrimply Delicious.* Garden City, N.Y.: Doubleday & Co., Inc.

Taylor, Herb (1975). *The Lobster: Its Life Cycle.* New York: Sterling Publishing Co., Inc.

Wall, Roy (1972). *Game and Fish from Field to Table.* San Antonio: The Naylor Co.

(1973). *Wonders of Alligators and Crocodiles.* New York: Dodd Mead & Co.

Wisner, Bill (1973). *How to Catch Saltwater Fish.* Garden City, N.Y.: Doubleday & Co., Inc.

Yonge, C.M. (1960). *Oysters.* London: Collins.

Notes

Category Index

Category Index

Category Index

Luncheon Dishes or Late Suppers

Category Index

Category Index

Main Courses

Category Index

Main Courses

Category Index

Notes

Index

A

B

Index

Index

290

Index

Index

F

G

Index

Index

Index

Index

Index

Index

Index

Index

Index

Index

How long the road is,
But for all the time the journey has already
taken
How you have needed every second of it
In order to learn what the road passes by.

Dag Hammarskjold

FAMOUS FLORIDA!™ RESTAURANTS & RECIPES: A collection of recipes that reveals the secrets behind the specialty dishes of 50 of Florida's top restaurants. Each restaurant review is accompanied by a description of the area, along with suggestions for day trips. Visitors who tour Florida by following the regional and culinary tips in FAMOUS FLORIDA!™ will discover a distinctive eating experience.

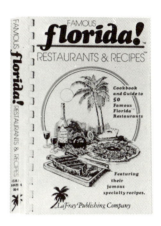

FAMOUS FLORIDA!™ Cracker Cookin' & Other Favorites:

What are some of the things Florida is most famous for?
    Alligators, oranges, Indians, Spanish and Cuban heritage, conch, and palm trees!
CRACKER COOKIN' is filled with these popular symbols of the Sunshine State. Here in one volume are vignettes of long-established back-roads eateries where Cracker favorites are served, together with instructions on how to prepare these dishes yourself.

As a combination cookbook/tour guide, CRACKER COOKIN' is an easy-to-use book, Ponce de Leon himself would ask for if he were here today.

Cook up a storm with these 150 easy-to-prepare down-home recipes for traditional Florida Cracker foods, Indian and Hispanic ethnic dishes, Southern home cookin', and other favorites.

Notes

Notes

Notes

Notes

Notes

Notes

Notes

311